DESIGNING ENVIRONMENTS

Christine V. Johnson

Nancy Cook, Project Director

Developed by Washington MESA

Funded by The Discuren Foundation

DALE SEYMOUR PUBLICATIONS®

Orangeburg, New York

Washington MESA wishes to express its appreciation to the following people for their advice and assistance, without which this module could not have been completed:

Nancy Cook, Ph.D.
Washington MESA
University of Washington
Seattle, Washington

Christine V. Johnson
Washington MESA
University of Washington
Seattle, Washington

Lee Copeland
Weinstein Copeland Architects
Seattle, Washington

Rolaine Copeland
Architecture in Education
American Institute of Architects
Seattle, Washington

Robert Lee
South Shore Middle School
Seattle, Washington

Monica Bergman
Voyager Middle School
Everett, Washington

Steve Regan
Toppenish Middle School
Toppenish, Washington

Susy Hagen
Washington Middle School
Yakima, Washington

Linda Este
Issac Stevens Middle School
Pasco, Washington

Brian Jaramillo
YVTC MESA
Pasco, Washington

Samantha Golliet
Komachin Middle School
Lacey, Washington

Linda Eich
Komachin Middle School
Lacey, Washington

Bobbe Haley
North Tapps Middle School
Sumner, Washington

Washington MESA Middle School Mathematics and Science Teachers in Inchelium, Mukilteo, Pasco, Seattle, Spokane, Tacoma, Toppenish, University Place, and Yakima, Washington

Project Editor: Joan Gideon
Production/Manufacturing: Joe Conte
Design Manager: Jeff Kelly
Text Design: Michelle Taverniti
Text Illustration: Carl Yoshihara
Cover Design: Dennis Teutschel
Cover Photograph: Harald Sund, The Image Bank

Drawing on page 14 reprinted courtesy of Hammond Beeby and Babka, Inc.
Photographs: page 85: reprinted by permission of Smith College Archives
page 65: photograph by Katherine Lambert
page 67: reprinted courtesy Susan Maxman Architects photograph by Tom Bernard
page 123: reprinted by permission Eric Krosnos

This book is published by Dale Seymour Publications®, an imprint of Addison Wesley Longman, Inc.

Dale Seymour Publications
125 Greenbush Road South
Orangeburg, NY 10962
Customer Service: 800-872-1100

Funded by the Discuren Foundation. This material in part is based on work supported by Grant No. MDR-8751287 from the National Science Foundation; Instructional Materials Development; Arlington, VA 22230. The material was designed and developed by Washington MESA (Mathematics, Engineering, Science Achievement); University of Washington; 353 Loew Hall Box 352181, Seattle, WA 98195-2181. Any opinions, findings, conclusions, or recommendations expressed in this publication are those of Washington MESA and do not necessarily reflect the views of the National Science Foundation.

Printed in the United States of America

ISBN 1-57232-917-3
DS 21854
1 2 3 4 5 6 7 8 9 10-ML-01 00 99 98 97

DESIGNING ENVIRONMENTS

CONTENTS

INTRODUCTION

Designing Environments is one of the middle-grades instructional modules created and field-tested by the Washington MESA (Mathematics, Engineering, Science Achievement) Middle School Curriculum Project. Washington MESA operates on the premise that effective classroom materials should facilitate connections between classroom and real-world mathematics and science. Staff members and teachers work with scientists, mathematicians, and engineers to outline each module. Pilot modules are tested in middle school classrooms, and then revised using feedback from the teachers.

The modules weave important mathematics themes with relevant, exciting science topics. The activities are based on current reform philosophies recommended by the National Council of Teachers of Mathematics *Curriculum and Evaluation Standards for School Mathematics* and the American Association for the Advancement of Science *Project 2061*. Students will

◆ learn by doing. Students follow architectural procedures as teams develop and revise floor plan designs, prepare cost estimates, and build a scale model of a cabin for a proposed middle school environmental camp.

◆ employ a variety of reasoning processes while using several mathematical approaches to solve similar problems.

◆ learn to express technical concepts as they write and discuss solutions to open-ended questions. The questions are designed to provoke further thought about how mathematics and science connect to the everyday world.

◆ learn the appropriate use of calculators by solving real problems. Students learn how to conceptualize and set up problems that they can then solve using calculators.

◆ make connections between mathematics and science as well as connections within mathematics and science. Writing Link, Technology Link, History Link, Career Link, and Interest Link pages are included to expand the connections to other subject areas by providing additional information.

◆ explore careers by assuming professional roles in the activities. Students also study professions that use mathematics and science in the Career Link features.

Designing Environments directs middle school students toward active involvement in learning. Students emulate real-world work environments by collaborating in small groups and striving for group consensus. They work with concrete materials and evaluate open-ended problems—the combination that helps the transition from concrete to abstract thinking that is crucial to the intellectual development of students at this age. To enable teachers to evaluate student's progress, assessment is integrated into *Designing Environments* activities. Assessment and instruction goals are identical.

Family encouragement can help students to succeed educationally, so a special activity involves students' families in hands-on, collaborative work. Students learn as they work with parents and other family members to design a neighborhood playhouse satisfying specific criteria.

Each activity begins with an Overview page summarizing what students will be doing and how the teacher needs to prepare. This is followed by background information for the teacher's use and a Presenting the Activity section, which describes the activity in detail and suggests discussion questions and assessment strategies. The activities also include Students Sheets and Transparency Masters in blackline master form (completed Student Sheets are provided on pages 129–140). Career Link, History Link, Writing Link, Technology Link, and Interest Link features are found throughout the module.

CONCEPTUAL OVERVIEW

Designing Environments addresses the following mathematics topics, science topics, and NCTM standards.

NCTM Curriculum Standards

Problem Solving
  Open-Ended
  Multiple Strategies
Communication
  Verbal and Written
Reasoning
  Logical and Spatial
  Predictions and Evaluations
Mathematical Connections
  Among Topics
  To Real-World Contexts

NCTM Teaching Standards

Worthwhile Tasks
  Real-World Contexts
Teacher's Role
  Listening and Observing
  Orchestrating Discourse
Enhancement Tools
  Calculators
  Concrete Materials
Learning Environment
  Collaborative Work

NCTM Evaluation Standards

Alignment
  Integral to Instruction
Multiple Sources
  Oral and Written
  Individual and Group
Multiple Methods
  Instructional Planning
  Grading
Mathematical Power
  Communicating
  Reasoning
  Integrating
  Generalizing

Mathematics Content

Number Relationships
  Ratios
  Decimals
  Ratio and Proportion
Computation and Estimation
  Mental Arithmetic
  Calculation
  Estimation
  Approximation
Functions and Relations
  Pattern Investigations
  Relations and Representations
Spatial Sense and Geometry
  Shape and Dimension
  Constructions
  Coordinate Grids
  Similarity

Measurement
  Dimension
  Perimeter
  Area
  Scale Drawings
  Angle Measures
  Estimation
  Units
  Tools
Statistics
  Data Analysis
  Inferences

Science Topics

Scientific Process
  Predicting
  Hypothesizing
  Analyzing
  Concluding
Environmental
  Animal Preserves
  Building Design
Architecture
  Floor Plans
  Exterior Walls
  Roofs
  Economics
  Models

ACTIVITY OVERVIEW

Overview

Middle school students are familiar with architecture in their environment as it appears in their homes, schools, neighborhoods, and city buildings. As a result, they may know that architecture deals with mathematical questions involving geometry, measurement, and computation. However, they are probably unfamiliar with how perimeter and area concepts can influence design decisions and cost factors. Students may understand the artistic aspects of a career in architecture; through this module, they will appreciate the additional role of an architect as a problem solver.

Designing Environments gives students a sampling of activities that develop the mathematics and methods architects use in design and construction. The module revolves around designing facilities for a middle school environmental camp and culminates with having each team build a scale model of their camp cabin. It focuses on the mathematics of design but does not address structural principles involving strength and stability. There are several excellent resources that focus primarily on this aspect of architecture that would complement this module. These include *Structures* by Bernie Zubrowski, and *The Art of Construction* by Mario Salvadori.

If possible, invite an architect to visit the class. She will be able to present specific examples, work with students on developing scale models, and answer questions concerning career opportunities in architecture.

Activity 1: Architecture and Design

Students design a cabin for a proposed 164-acre middle school environmental camp. After using architectural flow diagrams to arrange the living space, teams of two students design a preliminary floor plan to scale and estimate construction costs. Comparisons are then made among the different student designs, focusing on the areas, total costs, and costs per square foot. Based on this analysis, students explore how shape and size relate to cost and influence design decisions. Students begin to understand the role of an architect as a problem solver, and how the architect and client work together.

Activity 2: Pondering Perimeter

Students design the layout for a 40-acre animal preserve located at the environmental camp. They discover how perimeter can vary greatly for a given area, as well as how various shapes can have the same area and perimeter. Through a polyomino investigation, students develop strategies for using tiles to represent different perimeters. They use pattern recognition to write relationships for finding the minimum and maximum 40-omino perimeters. As a result, they determine all the perimeter possibilities for preserves made up of 40 square tiles. Teams examine a plot plan of the campsite, decide on the location for their animal preserve and cabins, and then determine how long it might take them to walk the preserve perimeter.

Activity 3: Accentuating Area

The exterior wall costs are identified as the most expensive aspect of construction. By revisiting the polyomino investigation to consider designs for a camp guest cottage with a fixed perimeter, students explore how limiting the amount of building materials affects area and design. Cottage building expenses are assessed, and data is graphed comparing floor area to cost and then floor area to cost per square foot. In this way, students examine construction issues such as which designs are the least expensive or the most cost-effective. Finally, they develop strategies for finding all the possible polyomino plans with an area of 8 square units and a perimeter of 14 units to identify cottage designs with equivalent construction costs. Through these scenarios, students confront the effect of shape on cost effectiveness and balance it with building appeal. They then use their insights to prepare a floor plan for a camp cottage, working within a limited budget.

Activity 4: Modifications and Models

Students develop an appreciation of the design process that takes the architectural team through a series of revisions toward the final solution and presentation model. They collaborate in groups of four, revising preliminary camp cabin designs from Activity 1 to prepare a final plan that incorporates the needs of the client while using area and perimeter relationships developed in previous activities. Each group builds a cardstock model of their cabin to assess its visual impact. They compile construction costs and write a short report detailing the features of their cabin.

Activity 5: Raising the Roof

After investigating roof pitch and its effect on aesthetics, cost, and function, students select a suitable pitch for their model and follow instructions to construct a simple gable roof. To recognize the effect different roof styles have on the appearance of a building, groups consider at least one other roof design appropriate for their cabin from the options provided before finalizing their presentation model.

Family Activity: Project Playhouse

Students are introduced to CASA (Court Appointed Special Advocates), an organization that provides representatives in court for abused and neglected children. CASA programs throughout the country auction or raffle off playhouses as an annual fundraising event. In this activity, each family brainstorms ideas, designs a children's playhouse, and builds a scale model of it with the intent of donating the design to CASA or a local organization of their choosing, which will auction off the completed playhouse to benefit their programs.

MATERIALS LIST

The following is a consolidated list of materials needed in *Designing Environments*. A list of materials needed for each activity is included in the Overview for each activity.

Activity	Materials Required
Architecture and Design	*For each student:* ◆ Student Sheets 1.1–1.4 ◆ Interest Link: The Hole-in-the-Wall Gang Camp *For each group of students:* ◆ Blank transparency ◆ Transparency pen ◆ Several sheets of $\frac{1}{4}$-inch grid paper ◆ Customary rulers ◆ Calculators *For the teacher:* ◆ 11 pennies per group (optional) ◆ $\frac{1}{2}$-inch transparency grid ◆ Transparency Masters 1.5–1.10 ◆ Transparencies of Student Sheets 1.1–1.4
Pondering Perimeter	*For each student:* ◆ Student Sheets 2.1–2.4 ◆ Interest Link: Species Survival Plan *For each group of students:* ◆ 80–100 square tiles ◆ Several sheets of $\frac{1}{4}$-inch grid paper ◆ Colored pens or pencils ◆ Calculators ◆ Customary rulers ◆ Scissors ◆ Clear tape ◆ $\frac{1}{4}$-inch transparency grid ◆ Yardstick or tape measure (optional)

Activity	Materials Required
	For the teacher: ◆ $\frac{1}{4}$-inch transparency grid ◆ Transparencies of Student Sheets 2.1–2.4
Accentuating Area	*For each student:* ◆ Student Sheets 3.1–3.3 ◆ Completed Student Sheet 2.3 ◆ Calculator ◆ Customary rulers *For each group of students:* ◆ Square tiles ◆ Several sheets of $\frac{1}{4}$-inch grid paper *For the teacher:* ◆ Several $\frac{1}{4}$-inch transparency grids ◆ Transparencies of Student Sheets 3.1–3.3
Modifications and Models	*For each student:* ◆ Student Sheets 4.1–4.2 *For each group of students:* ◆ Cabin floor plans from Activity 1 ◆ Calculators ◆ Several sheets of $\frac{1}{4}$-inch grid paper ◆ Customary rulers ◆ 4–6 sheets of $8\frac{1}{2}$-inch by 11-inch cardstock ◆ Clear tape ◆ Scissors ◆ X-Acto® knife (optional) ◆ 9-inch by 12-inch manila envelopes (optional) *For the teacher:* ◆ Transparencies of Student Sheets 4.1–4.2 ◆ List of student responses from Activity 1 on the role of mathematics in architecture
Raising the Roof	*For each student:* ◆ Student Sheets 5.1–5.3 *For each group of students:* ◆ Calculators ◆ Several sheets of grid paper ◆ Customary rulers ◆ 5–6 sheets of $8\frac{1}{2}$-inch by 11-inch cardstock ◆ Clear tape ◆ Scissors ◆ Protractor or Cuisenaire® angle ruler

Activity	Materials Required
Raising the Roof	*For the teacher:* ◆ Transparency Master 5.4 ◆ Transparencies of Student Sheets 5.1–5.3
Project Playhouse	*For each student:* ◆ Interest Link: CASA: An Advocate for Children ◆ Family Activity Sheets 1–2 *For each family:* ◆ $\frac{1}{4}$-inch grid paper ◆ Paper for drawings ◆ Cardstock for the model ◆ Scissors ◆ Tape ◆ Ruler ◆ Calculator ◆ X-Acto® knife ◆ 12-inch by 12-inch cardboard base *For the teacher:* ◆ Transparencies of Family Activity Sheets 1–2

RESOURCES LIST

This list of resources was compiled by teachers, scientists, and profession-als who participated in developing *Designing Environments*. It is intended for teachers who would like to pursue the topic further, either with their class, with small groups of students who are particularly interested in the topic, with individual students who desire further investigations, or as part of their professional development.

1. The American Institute of Architects (AIA)
   1735 New York Avenue, NW
   Washington, DC 20006-5292
   202-626-7300

2. The AIA Career in Architecture Video Program. "Career Encounters: Architecture." Davis Gray Inc., 1992.

3. American Zoo and Aquarium Association
   Executive Office and Conservation Center
   7970-D Old Georgetown Road
   Bethesda, Maryland 20814
   301-907-7777

4. *Architecture in Education*. Edited by M. Abhau, R. Copeland, and G. Greenberger. Philadelphia: Foundation for Architecture, 1986.

5. "Hammond Beeby and Babka Hole-in-the-Wall Gang Camp, Connecticut." *Architectural Design* 59, No. 9–10 (1988): 70–73.

6. The National Court Appointed Special Advocate Association (CASA)
   100 West Harrison Street
   North Tower, Suite 500
   Seattle, Washington 98119-4123
   800-628-3233

7. *Notes on Architecture.* Developed by L. Belliston. Los Altos, California: William Kaufmann, Inc., 1982.

8. Blackwell, William. *Architecture in Geometry.* Berkeley: Key Curriculum Press, 1984.

9. Cole, Doris. *From Tipi to Skyscraper.* Boston: I Press, Inc., 1973.

10. Polakowski, Kenneth. *Zoo Design: The Reality of Wild Illusions.* The University of Michigan School of Natural Resources, 1987.

11. Salvadori, Mario. *The Art of Construction.* Chicago: Chicago Review Press, Inc., 1990.

12. Stein, Karen. "New Frontier." *Architectural Record* (January 1989): 86–91.

13. Walter, Marion. *Boxes, Squares, and Other Things.* Washington, DC: National Council of Teachers of Mathematics, 1970.

14. Zubrowski, Bernie. *Structures.* New York: Cuisenaire Company of America, Inc., 1993.

ACTIVITY
1

ARCHITECTURE AND DESIGN

Overview

Students design a cabin for a 164-acre environmental camp. After using architectural flow diagrams to show possible arrangements of the living space, teams of two students design a floor plan to scale and estimate construction costs. Comparisons are then made among the different student designs, focusing on the areas, total costs, and costs per square foot. Students begin to understand the role of an architect as a problem solver, and how the architect and client work together.

Time. Three to four 45-minute periods.

Purpose. Students recognize the issues involved in designing a floor plan to fit human needs. By comparing cabin costs, students explore how shape and size relate to cost and influence design decisions.

Materials. *For each student:*

◆ Student Sheets 1.1–1.4

◆ Interest Link: The Hole-in-the-Wall Gang Camp

For each group of students:

◆ Blank transparency

◆ Transparency pen

◆ Several sheets of $\frac{1}{4}$-inch grid paper

◆ Customary rulers

◆ Calculators

For the teacher:

◆ 11 pennies per group (optional)

◆ $\frac{1}{2}$-inch transparency grid

◆ Transparency Masters 1.5–1.10

◆ Transparencies of Student Sheets 1.1–1.4

Getting Ready

1. Gather the necessary materials and tools listed above and have them available for students. Grid paper may be photocopies from page 142.

2. Duplicate Student Sheets 1.1–1.4.

3. Prepare a $\frac{1}{2}$-inch transparency grid (page 143).

4. Prepare Transparency Masters 1.5–1.10.

5. Prepare transparencies of Student Sheets 1.1–1.4.

Background Information

Architecture is only one of the many elements in our environment, but it is one of the most important. Architecture molds the places we live, learn, and work. Architects are concerned with achieving and preserving quality in the environment. What is built, why it is built, and where it is built are all part of the profession's responsibility. The architect, in collaboration with the client, strives to achieve an architecture of consequence. The Roman architect Marcus Vitruvius Pollio believed,

> A building must meet the following standards to qualify as architecture: it must conveniently serve the purpose for which it was built, it must be structurally sound, and it must be beautiful. (Pollio. *The Ten Books on Architecture*. Translated by M. H. Morgan. Cambridge: Harvard University Press, 1914.)

These three factors—use, construction, and aesthetics—are always present and interrelated. It is impossible for the architect to think of one of them without considering the other two as well. Decisions regarding any one of them will inevitably affect the others.

Every architect is a problem solver. The recurring problem is to create aesthetically pleasing architecture while at the same time meeting the client's needs. All architectural design begins with a purpose and goes through a series of problem-solving experiences to address various constraints. Each activity in this unit follows this concept while exploring the inherent mathematics.

Architecture and geometry are inseparable. Understanding the properties and relations of lines, patterns, surfaces, and solids is vital to an architect. Students use mathematics in this activity to design a camp cabin. They are given a problem to solve with design specifications and implied financial constraints—to produce innovative yet practical cabin designs for a proposed middle school environmental camp. In teams of two, they design a floor plan to scale and use the area of the floor as well as the perimeter of the base to estimate construction costs.

An architect's first designs for a project are called *drafts*. Further analysis leads to the final floor plan and presentation model. In this same way, students propose their initial ideas and complete subsequent activities in this module to enhance their understanding of area and perimeter concepts. In Activity 5, teams of four students propose final camp cabin designs and presentation models.

A site survey of the 164-acre environmental camp is provided on Transparency Master 1.5. The scale is $\frac{1}{2}$-inch square = 1 acre, or 43,560 square feet. The curving lines are the contours. The elevation changes by 5 feet between two adjacent contour lines. The contours show how the land is gradually sloping downward from the northwest corner toward the lake area, and then rising again as you move toward the east.

The Hole-in-the-Wall Gang Camp Interest Link along with Transparency Master 1.6 may be used as an example of what architects have done in a similar situation. It is a 300-acre rural summer camp in northeastern Connecticut for children with life-threatening diseases. The camp was envisioned by Paul Newman and designed by the architectural firm of Hammond Beeby and Babka of Chicago. Many of the mathematical ideas this module addresses are found in the designs of this camp.

During the initial planning stage, architects sketch a series of flow diagrams before considering a floor plan. Circular shapes are sketched to determine the general location of each room in the building. The size of each shape corresponds to the relative sizes of the proposed rooms. Arrows show room connections and possible doorways. Examining flow diagrams for the proposed three-room cabin reveals numerous arrangements, such as the ones illustrated below.

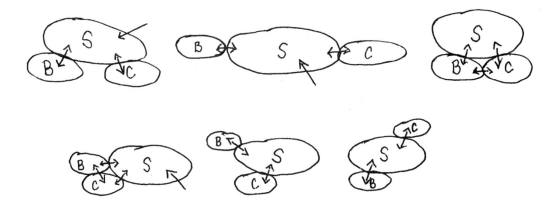

S = Student Sleeping Area; C = Counselor's Room; B = Bathroom

Selecting the desired flow diagram leads naturally into preparing a floor plan with detailed information on the size and shape of each room. The same uniform scale used by architects ($\frac{1}{4}$ in. = 1 ft) is applied to students designs and models. If you have an architect's scale (a ruler with several scales including one that converts a $\frac{1}{4}$-inch scale into feet), show students how easily they can draw and read scale plans by using this tool. Or you could ask an architect visiting the class to bring and demonstrate the architect's scale.

When students are designing floor plans, they must use scale and proportion to make the designs functional. For example, rooms must be sized appropriately for furniture or bathroom facilities, doors must have free space to open, and aisles must be wide enough for people to pass. In other words, the space must be livable.

The floor plan provides enough information to estimate construction costs. Roof expense estimates are provided, even though at this stage the plans are developed without roofs. The expense estimates include materials and labor costs that are realistic at the time of publication. The expenses for floors and roofs are based on area; those for walls are based on perimeter. Expense rates are listed below.

Expense Estimates

Structure	Cost
Floors	$ 9.75 per square foot
10-Foot-High Exterior Walls	$140.00 per linear foot
10-Foot-High Interior Walls	$35.00 per linear foot
Roof	1.5 times the floor cost

Floor costs include joists, beams, a subfloor, and a finished hardwood floor. Exterior walls assume 2-by-6 studs (boards that measured 2 inches by 6 inches before they were seasoned and planed), sheeting, insulation, gypsum board inside and cedar shingles outside with a 4-foot-high, 6-inch-thick reinforced concrete foundation. Interior walls have 2-by-4 studs with gypsum board on both sides. Exposed surfaces are painted.

Wall height can influence cost. Ten-foot cabin walls are initially suggested to eliminate height as a variable. This gives students an opportunity to observe that when base perimeters differ, costs can vary for cabins with the same area. For example, a cabin with an area of 540 square feet can have many possible shapes, including those pictured on page 5. Though each cabin contains the same interior room spaces—270-square-foot camper area, 120-square-foot counselor room, and 150-square-foot bathroom facility—their differing perimeters affect the exterior wall costs.

Cabin Plans

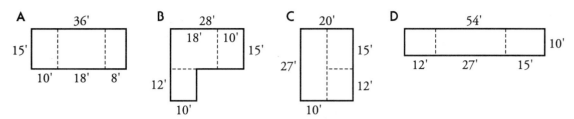

Cabin Perimeters

	A	B	C	D
Perimeter (ft)	102	110	94	128

Multiplying each cabin perimeter by the $140 exterior wall estimate provides the range of wall costs listed in the table below. Final costs are rounded to the nearest dollar.

Cost Estimates

Structure	A	B	C	D
Floor	$5,265	$5,265	$5,265	$5,265
Exterior Walls	$14,280	$15,400	$13,160	$17,920
Interior Walls	$1,050	$875	$1,295	$700
Roof	$7,898	$7,898	$7,898	$7,898
Total Cost	$28,493	$29,438	$27,618	$31,783

Though a $1,000 total cost difference may seem inconsequential, when multiplied by a total of 15 cabins, the savings becomes $15,000. A $2,000 total cost difference represents a $30,000 savings, which is more than the cost of one cabin.

Some designs may cost excessive amounts or may not suit the physical needs of the campers. For example, the sleeping areas in C and D may be inadequate to fit the intended bunk beds for ten campers. Notice also how D is simply the result of moving the two smaller rooms of C to the ends of the larger room. The effect is an increase in perimeter that corresponds to additional exterior wall and foundation expenses.

A square cabin with an area of 540 square feet has a perimeter of approximately 93 feet (4 × 23.2 ft). For about 3 more feet of perimeter, one can build a 24-feet-by-24-feet cabin, gaining 36 square feet of additional living space. This larger square cabin costs approximately one percent less to build than model B and about one percent more than model A.

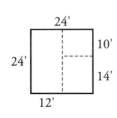

Cost Estimates for Cabin E

Floor	$5,616
Exterior Walls	$13,440
Interior Walls	$1,260
Roof	$8,424
Total Cost	**$28,740**

The square footage of the cabins designed by the students may vary greatly. For this reason, comparing the costs per square foot as well as the overall costs provides more accurate information on cost-effectiveness. Cost per square foot relates to the cost-effectiveness of a design. As the cost per square foot of a design decreases, its cost-effectiveness increases. The cost estimates per square foot for cabins A–E above are listed below. They have been determined by dividing the total costs by the area of the interior living space and rounding to the nearest dollar.

Cabin Cost per Square Foot

A	B	C	D	E
$53	$55	$51	$59	$50

The information on cost per square foot indicates cabin E is about $3 per square foot cheaper to build than cabin A, though their total costs are approximately the same. The overall cost to build cabin E is about $1,000 more than the cost of cabin C; yet cabin E costs approximately $1 per square foot less to build!

Some students may propose very large, yet cost-effective cabin designs. A balance between cost-effectiveness and size is important. An expensive, yet highly cost-effective design with excessive square footage beyond the client's need is no more desirable than a less-expensive one with adequate square footage.

These comparisons accentuate the architect's dilemma of how to balance concerns about functionality, aesthetics, and cost. The concept of maximizing living space while using a minimum amount of building material is introduced within this activity and becomes a recurring theme throughout the module.

The evaluation of student work in this module is to be based on the development of their ideas, not on the choices made regarding whether to minimize the amount of material used in construction. Architectural design is certainly an area where one approach does not always prevail, nor will any group of architects necessarily agree on what constitutes the criteria for judging design decisions. Instead, the basis for assessment ought to be primarily on the development and use of the mathematical concepts presented, and secondly on the quality of the constructed model. Students must acquire an adequate understanding of the mathematics necessary in order to be able to make informed decisions concerning their designs and models.

Student Sheets 1.1–1.2 provide a scenario for the proposed environmental camp and put students in the role of an architect, discussing design possibilities for a camp cabin that meets the client's approval. The subsequent interactions and group decisions illustrate how the architect and the client work together. Architects can use their imagination to design anything they want, but if they cannot find a client to appreciate their creation, it will never be built.

You may want to consider certain cabin criteria and, when appropriate, field questions from your students that would be normally directed toward the client. The basic requirements are for three rooms: a campers' sleeping area, a counselor's room, and a bathroom. The layout of each area must provide sufficient space for furniture, bathroom facilities, circulation, and storage. Keeping the general scenario in mind, you will need to rely on your own judgment for those unforeseen questions, though some guidelines are suggested in the section Presenting the Activity. Your responses should focus on specific details and not pass judgment on the aesthetic appeal of a particular design.

Before finalizing cabin designs and preparing floor plans, students decide on the furniture and facilities necessary for each room and research actual measurements as homework.

Prior to completing Student Sheet 1.2, each team determines the square footage of their proposed cabin and lists the design aspects that address the client's needs as well as those that make their cabin appealing. On Student Sheet 1.3, teams assess construction costs, including the cost per square foot, before presenting their plans to the group.

It is through working on shape, size, and costs on Student Sheet 1.4 that students begin to think about the relationships among these factors.

Use the Career Link "An Architect" any time during the activity to enhance student interest.

Presenting the Activity

Architecture. Begin the activity by asking student groups to discuss what they know about architecture. Why does it exist? Where does it exist? Who is responsible for it? Orchestrate a class discussion to elicit their responses. As students realize that the influence of architecture exists within every type of building within a community and that it has the ability to inspire us through its aesthetics, they may conclude that aspects of architecture exist everywhere and that a wide variety of people engage in architectural work, from trained professionals to ordinary people.

Have students discuss what they think the role of mathematics is in architecture. During class discussion, list their ideas on the board or overhead while students provide examples to substantiate them. Mention that other mathematical ideas may be added to this list as activities in this module are completed. Conclude by saying that mathematics can exist without architecture, but architecture cannot exist without mathematics. Keep a copy of the list for future use in Activity 4.

Camp Cabins. Have student groups discuss what is meant by the statement that all architecture begins with a purpose. Consider their interpretations before distributing Student Sheet 1.1 to each student. Provide time for them to read the opening scenario and to discuss it with their groups before you conduct a class discussion to summarize the intent.

Display the site survey on Transparency Master 1.5. Discuss the site shape and slope, pointing out the lake and streams feeding into it. Use a $\frac{1}{2}$-inch transparency grid as an overlay to illustrate the scale of the survey as it relates to the 164 acres. Answer any questions as necessary to clarify the features of the site.

Use the Interest Link (page 14) and Transparency Master 1.6 to introduce the Hole-in-the-Wall Gang Camp. Talk about the circumstances behind its conception and development as an example of the process that an architect goes through when working with a client and making design decisions. Explain that part of the design process includes discussions with the client to answer specific questions that arise during the initial planning stage. While brainstorming design possibilities, any questions students have for the client should be listed.

As students resume work on Student Sheet 1.1, move from group to group, taking part in planning discussions when appropriate. Some questions you may want to resolve later with class input, others you may decide to field within the group, while a few may require an immediate response to the whole class.

If students inquire about cost issues, you may ask what design aspects influence cost. Cost is a consideration, but the cabin should satisfy the client's needs. Students may ask about size. A response may indicate no oversized cabins, yet the campers should not feel cramped. Does it have to be rectangular? No, but that is a possibility. If they ask how large to make each room, answer that they must decide, with the understanding that size can affect livability as well as aesthetics and cost. Remind them that the client will be choosing one of the class cabin designs, and that both cost and functionality will be factors. Tell students the camp will provide a separate dining and social hall. Each team should decide whether to include a fireplace or wood stove, depending on their assessment of environmental and aesthetic issues. Students need not consider overall heating requirements otherwise for purposes of this activity.

During follow-up discussions, focus on the use and variety of flow diagrams. Ask them how many different cabin representations are possible. As they conclude that the variety is endless, inquire as to which flow diagrams might be more appealing from the camper's point of view and why. Have students consider the counselor's point of view as well. Bring out how point of view varies according to each person's perspective and the influence this has on design decisions.

Ask why they think weather information is given in the introduction. They may realize weather can influence not only the design, but also the building materials used in construction, which can affect cost. Inquire as to which design decisions they feel belong to the architect, and which to the client. (Decisions involving building codes, safety codes, or structural integrity, and consideration of what is actually buildable are the type of decisions left for the architect.)

Before class ends, ascertain that groups understand which furniture or building measurements they may need before determining which room dimensions will meet human needs. Be sure that students know ways to research these measurements. Some possibilities include: measuring their own beds and furniture; measuring bathroom stalls and sinks at school; calling architects, local camps, or furniture stores to get the needed information.

Dwelling Designs. Have student groups consider these questions: What is a floor plan? What information does a floor plan give? How would you design one?

Distribute Student Sheet 1.2 and give each group a blank transparency along with a transparency pen. Provide students time to read the introduction along with questions 1 and 2 and discuss these in their groups. Then suggest each group imagine possible floor plans that might be represented by the flow diagram in question 2 and sketch them onto the transparency. Be sure students recognize that the flow diagram does not indicate the size or shape of the room. As you circulate among the groups, listen to the kinds of questions that come up and how the students resolve them, before intervening. It is important that students realize the floor plan determines the shape of the cabin. If groups continue to struggle, consider making a list of questions generated from each group. Have the class decide how to address them. This could include input from other groups, teacher responses, and researching ideas from other sources.

As groups finish their drawings, have them display their floor plans on the overhead and point out similarities and differences as well as how they indicated doorway and window locations. Show the architectural symbols used on Transparency 1.8 as one possibility. How are architectural drawings similar to and different from the student drawings? Use this presentation time to agree on uniform symbols to illustrate walls, doors, and windows.

Also talk about the variety of possible plans based on a single flow diagram. Transparency Master 1.7 may be used to provide additional examples of floor plans. Ask students which, if any, of these plans could have been based on the flow diagram in question 1.

If scale has not already been discussed, ask the class how scale is used in representing a floor plan. Within this discussion, explain that architects in this country use customary units of measurement, whereas in other countries, they use metric units. Inform students that a scale of $\frac{1}{4}$ inch = 1 foot is consistent with most architectural situations and will be used in this activity.

Distribute grid paper as students resume work on Student Sheet 1.2. At some point in their discussions, encourage groups to break into two teams. Each is to prepare a floor plan for the group to preview. As you move among the groups, encourage them to demonstrate that the spaces they have designed are adequate and not excessive. Suggest students consider using flat paper shapes to represent such things as beds, lockers or storage areas, and sinks. This will help them determine dimensions, organize the rooms, and verify livability. Have the groups discuss and decide how much space a person needs to move around comfortably and explain their reasoning. Elicit from the students suggestions of what might be used as a model to represent this space using the one-quarter-inch-equals-one-foot scale. If a penny is not one of the suggestions, explain that it can be used to represent a three-foot circle, the space that a person needs to move around comfortably. Suggest groups measure a penny to concur. You may want to give each group 11 pennies to see if they easily fit on their plan along with the furniture.

Be sure students notice that each interior wall serves two rooms at once, so that a change in one room makes a change in adjoining rooms. Observe their procedures for determining square footage and ask individuals to present their methods during follow-up discussions. Provide group time for teams to share finalized floor plans.

Expense Estimates. As teams complete their floor plans, they can begin working on Student Sheet 1.3 in class. Have student groups discuss their procedures for estimating expenses. Provide time for teams to demonstrate different yet valid methods to the class. At the same time, teams could present their method of calculating cost per square foot and explain why this information might be useful to the client. Questions 4–6 may be completed for homework.

Once groups have had a chance to discuss the benefits of saving $1,000 in construction costs per cabin, as well as whether comparing overall costs is a fair assessment of value, facilitate a class discussion to allow students to voice opinions. Ascertain how knowing the cost per square foot affects their preferences among cabin designs at this point.

Money Matters. Collect the necessary data on Transparency Masters 1.9 and 1.10, while students record it on Student Sheet 1.4. Allow time for groups to analyze the information, discuss the results, and respond to the questions. Clarify that your assessment of student work is based on team effort and the appropriate use of mathematical procedures, not on whether they have the best design. After collecting the necessary data in class, questions 2–9 may be completed for homework. Explain to students that they will have time in class to discuss question 8 in their groups the next day.

To view the floor plans, have students display them in the classroom, arranged according to cost. Begin a class discussion by asking if the order seems reasonable. Based on student reactions, some teams may need to verify cost calculations. When accurate expenses are established, ask which of the designs they believe the client might choose, and why.

Provide a forum for students to argue the merits of different plans. If appropriate, pursue their thinking on whether cabins with the same square footage, but different shapes, will cost the same to build. As they notice possible discrepancies, some may begin to suspect a relationship with perimeter. At this point, accept their thoughts, and allow them to ponder the situation for future discussions.

Find out if they think arranging the class cabins according to cost per square foot will affect the order. After assessing this question, have them rearrange the floor plans based on cost per square foot. Any surprises? Again, some teams may be asked to check their calculations. Ask student groups to list common characteristics among cabins with a low cost per square foot and then to list what those with a high cost per square foot have in common.

Conclude by reminding them this is their first draft toward a final cabin design. Tell them that in the next activities they will examine the ideas introduced here in more detail. Mention that in Activity 5, groups of four will collaborate to present a final floor plan and to build a model of their cabin.

Discussion Questions

1. What decisions are involved in designing a structure?
2. How does the size of your cabin compare with the size of your classroom?
3. What is an estimate of the average cost for the various cabin designs?
4. Wall height is a design factor.
    a. If a 10-foot-high wall section costs $140, what would an 8-foot-high section cost? (Though students may use a proportion to answer this question, in reality, some costs do not change when you make a wall higher, so the cost could be more than $112.)
    b. Would lowering the wall height of the cabins to 8 feet have the same cost effect on each cabin? Give examples to support your response.
5. Why do you think architects make more than one design for each project?

Assessment Questions

1. One architect designed a 60-square-unit rectangular floor plan to represent a 600-square-foot cabin.
    a. On grid paper, sketch possible 60-square-unit rectangular floor plans with unit dimensions. List the possible unit dimensions and label each rectangle appropriately.

b. Which cabin design(s) are the most livable? Explain your reasoning.

c. Which cabin design(s) are probably not livable? Explain your reasoning.

d. Which cabin seems to be the most economical to build? Explain your reasoning.

e. Which of the cabin designs do you prefer? Explain.

f. Which design(s) might the client prefer? Explain.

2. The client wants to build the cabin your team designed, but wants the price reduced by $2,000. Describe a way to alter your design that lowers the cost by $2,000.

3. Analyze the data you collected on costs.

a. What is the mean cost for the various class cabins?

b. What is the median cost of the class cabins?

c. Round each class cabin cost to the nearest $1,000 and make a bar graph to display the information. Describe what it shows.

The Hole-in-the-Wall Gang Camp

The Hole-in-the-Wall Gang Camp is a summer camp for children with life-threatening diseases. Located on 300 acres in northeastern Connecticut, it was envisioned by Paul Newman and designed by Hammond Beeby and Babka of Chicago.

The purpose of the Hole-in-the-Wall Gang Camp is to provide a full outdoor experience for those who would normally be denied that possibility by the nature of their physical needs. The architectural firm based their designs on these special needs of the client. The design provides campers with an an old-fashioned camp experience and the latest in medical care, while avoiding a sense of institution. The project design incorporates all the elements of a community in miniature. Its site plan is based on historical plans of the traditional American small town. The individual building elements intend to represent the various communal and private functions of such a settlement: a dining hall, a meeting place, and the cabins where campers sleep.

Initially, the architects explored two alternative planning options—a centralized facility housed in a minimum of buildings, and its antithesis, a decentralized layout of small structures scattered around the property's perimeter. Neither option suited the complex demands of the particular community. The town model represents the compromise between a rural image and the need for close supervision, and also embodies the American West theme that fit the contours of the site and intrigued both architect and client.

The public buildings of the camp include a 15-sided dining hall, an arc-roofed gymnasium, and a trio of interconnected arts-and-crafts classrooms. These form a casual perimeter of the town green. The director's quarters and apartments for medical staff occupy paired timber towers, which serve as symbolic gate houses to camper quarters. The log cabins are grouped in five clusters of three, surrounding a shared campfire.

The Hole-in-the-Wall Gang Camp serves as a hideaway from the institutions that govern these campers' lives. The health of the children who enroll in the camp is a serious issue, and the camp environment is purposefully pleasing.

An Architect

If you want a challenging profession, the opportunity for self-expression, the chance to see your ideas take shape, and the knowledge that what you create will endure, then you might want to consider becoming an architect.

An architect must have a wide range of abilities, such as the capability to draw and to convey ideas, as well as to visualize entire buildings. An architect is open-minded, enjoys solving mathematical problems, has an understanding of the building process, and has a creative imagination. A large part of the satisfaction you will get from architecture ultimately comes from turning your ideas into reality.

An architect designs buildings, draws up plans for their construction, and makes sure that the work is done well. As an architect, you will work with imposed financial restraints, balancing them with aesthetics while seeking the optimal building solutions. You must understand the complex topic of materials so you will know when a building should be built of wood and when it should be built of concrete. You must understand structural engineering to make certain that the building's design provides adequate strength and stability—for example, what loads different materials may safely carry, so that there will be no danger of the building falling down. You will coordinate a team of consultants, including contractors, engineers, interior designers, landscape architects, carpenters, surveyors, and building inspectors.

After completing a professional degree in architecture, you will have an internship period for practical experience while preparing to take the Architect Registration Examination test. After passing the test, you will become a licensed architect.

In a small architectural firm, you may perform different functions ranging from designing buildings to administering contracts, running an office, and controlling finances. In a large firm or in public service, you may have the opportunity to specialize in a particular type of building, such as factories, offices, apartments, hospitals, or houses.

An architect is not just concerned with buildings, but with improving the environment. You will have a role in social and environmental change, and must balance the needs of the client with public interest and the needs of the greater community.

Camp Cabins

A client planning to build a year-round environmental camp for middle school students is asking your architectural firm to submit design plans for a one-story cabin that sleeps ten campers. It should include a bathroom with two toilets, four sinks and two showers, as well as a separate private sleeping area for the cabin counselor. Your client wants to provide campers with a pleasant yet simple and rustic structure that emphasizes the outdoor experience.

The 164-acre, gently sloping wooded site has two streams draining into a small lake for nonmotorized recreation. The weather in fall and spring can be cool and damp, while summers are moderately hot. Light snowfall and wind are common in winter with temperatures generally above 20 degrees Fahrenheit.

As with all clients, keeping finances reasonable is a concern. Once they choose a design, they plan to build fifteen identical cabins so that 150 students can attend each session. They want a cabin that suits their needs, is aesthetically pleasing, and gives them the most for their money.

1. An architect must consider the basic needs that a design will fulfill. With your group, determine the number of rooms to include in the cabin design and explain the purpose of each one.

2. Architects use flow diagrams to show the general location of each room in a very rough form. These drawings use circular shapes to illustrate design ideas. One possibility is shown for a three-room cabin. Sketch a variety of flow diagrams to record possible cabin room arrangements for your client.

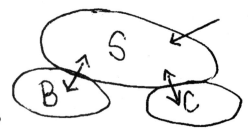

Camp Cabins

3. With your group, discuss the advantages and disadvantages of each flow diagram. Narrow your decision to two that seem to work best and use them as models for further development.

4. During this initial planning phase, write down any questions for the client that you may have.

5. Make a list of the specific measurements you will need to research before preparing your cabin plans. These may include dimensions of beds, lockers or storage areas for campers' clothing, doors, windows, and bathroom stalls. Decide who will be responsible for researching each measurement.

Dwelling Designs

A *floor plan* is a scale drawing. It is the view you would see if you cut the roof off of a building and looked down on the rooms from above. A floor plan shows the layout of each room and often how it is furnished. Including the furniture gives a better indication of the size of the room. A floor plan is used in estimating costs and in the actual construction of a building.

1. With your group, sketch onto a transparency possible floor plans that this flow diagram could represent.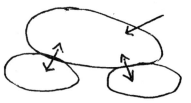
   a. How many different designs based on this flow diagram are possible? Explain.

   b. How did you indicate doorways in your sketches?

   c. How did you show window locations in your sketches?

2. Divide into two teams. List the members of each team. Each team will select one of your preferred flow diagrams from question 3 on Student Sheet 1.1 and create a cabin floor plan, following the instructions below. The group will preview both plans.

3. Use grid paper to draw the floor plan for your proposed cabin. Let $\frac{1}{4}$ inch = 1 foot. Be sure to indicate the cabin dimensions along the perimeter and draw to scale the location of doorways, windows, furniture, and bathroom facilities.

Dwelling Designs

4. Describe the shape of your cabin design. Explain why you selected this shape.

5. Determine the square footage of your cabin and explain your procedures.

6. List several reasons why the camp client should choose your design.

Expense Estimates

Expense Estimates

Structure	Cost
Floors	$ 9.75 per square foot
10-Foot-High Exterior Walls	$140.00 per linear foot
10-Foot-High Interior Walls	$35.00 per linear foot
Roof	1.5 times the floor cost

The exterior wall construction expenses include the cost of a concrete foundation. Window and door expenses are also considered part of the wall costs.

1. Use the above estimates to approximate the total cost for constructing your proposed cabin. Round final costs to the nearest dollar. Clearly describe your procedures.

2. Based on your calculations, the camp client will be charged approximately $_____ for the materials and labor necessary to build one cabin and $_____ for a total of fifteen camp cabins.

3. Compare the costs of the two building designs created by your group and describe the results.

4. If one cabin costs $1,000 more to build than another, is this a significant difference? Explain your reasoning.

Expense Estimates

5. Is it fair to compare overall costs to determine which cabin is the better buy? Explain your reasoning.

6. Another way to compare cabin costs is to analyze the expenses per square foot.
   a. Calculate the cost per square foot of floor space for your cabin design, and explain your procedures.

   b. How does the cost per square foot for your design compare to the cost per square foot of the other design in your group?

   c. Do the total cost and the cost per square foot give the same comparison? Explain your reasoning.

Money Matters

1. Record the expense estimates and the square footage for the cabin designs created by each team.

Class Cabin Costs

Team	Square Footage	Cost per Cabin	Cost of 15 Cabins	Cost per Square Foot
1.				
2.				
3.				
4.				
5.				
6.				
7.				
8.				
9.				
10.				
11.				
12.				
13.				
14.				
15.				
16.				

2. Based on the data for building the cabins designed by your class, determine
   a. the range of square footage
   b. the range of costs for 1 cabin
   c. the range of costs for 15 cabins
   d. the range of costs per square foot.

Money Matters

3. Are the expense differences significant? Explain your reasoning.

4. Will buildings with the same square footage always cost the same? Explain.

5. According to the table, does a larger cabin always cost more than a smaller cabin? Provide examples to support your reasoning.

6. What are possible causes for the variation in cabin expenses?

7. How many of the proposed cabin designs will cost the client more than your design? Less than your design?

8. Make a scatter plot of the class cabin data that relates the cost of each cabin to the square feet it provides. With your group, discuss what it shows, and then record your observations.

9. Are there any design changes you could make to increase the chance of your cabin being selected?

10. Besides cost, what else might influence the client's choice?

Site Survey

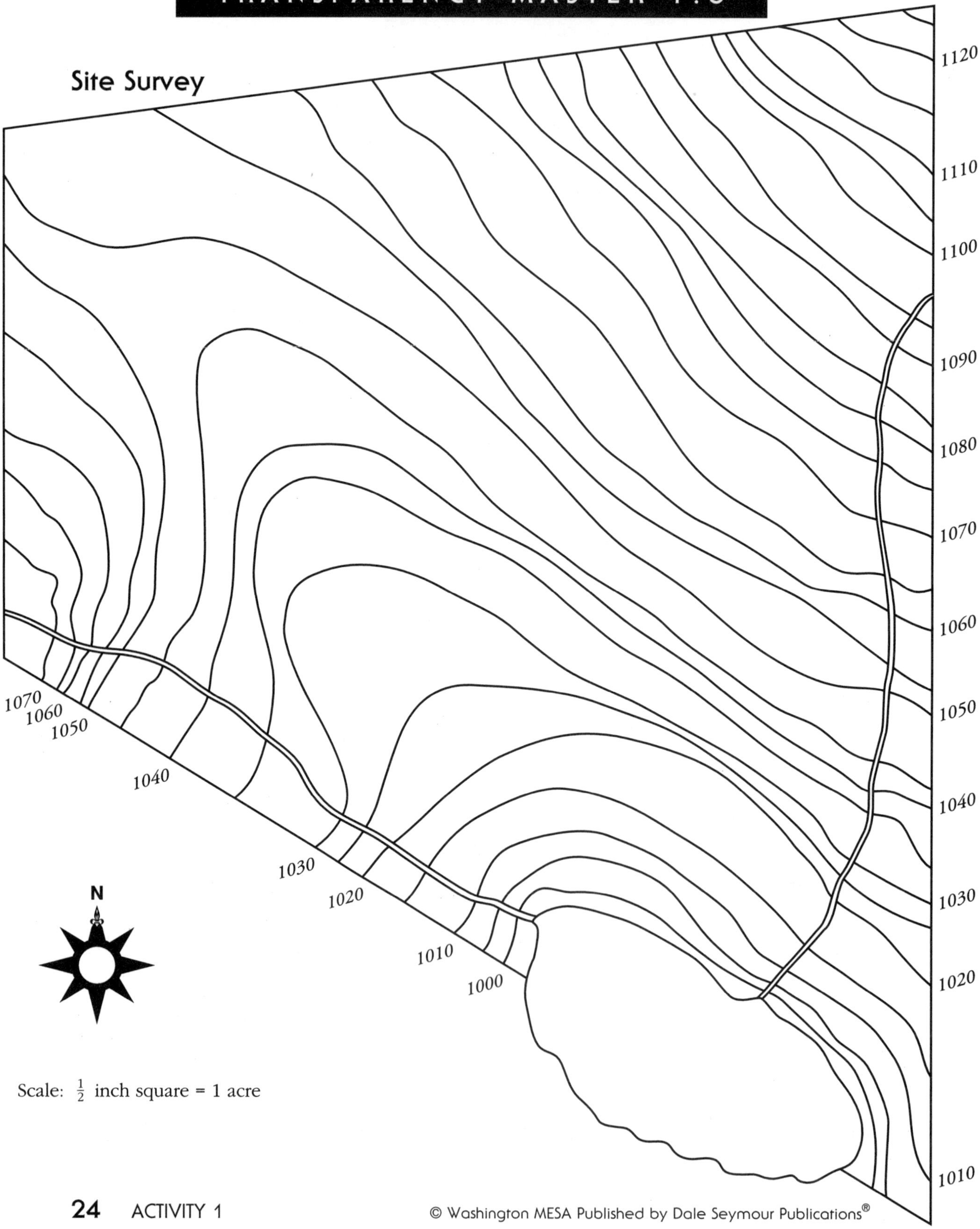

1120

1110

1100

1090

1080

1070

1060

1050

1040

1030

1020

1010

1070
1060
1050
1040
1030
1020
1010
1000

N

Scale: $\frac{1}{2}$ inch square = 1 acre

The Hole-in-the-Wall Gang Camp

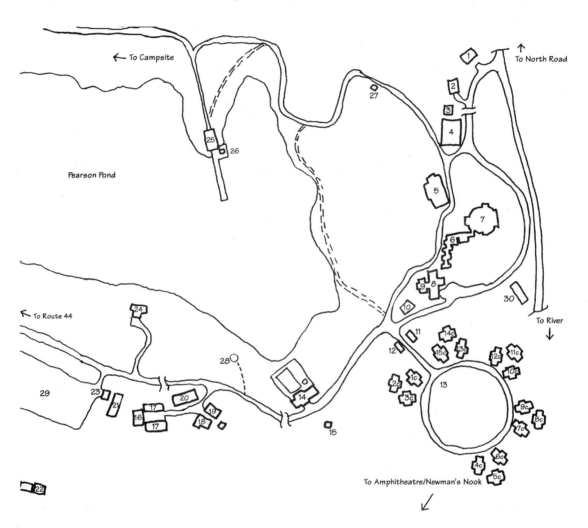

KEY

1.	Brown House
2.	Staff Barn
3.	Nature Hut
4.	Theater
5.	Gym
6.	Library/Arts & Crafts
7.	Dining Hall
8.	Infirmary
9.	Nurse/Doctor Lodging
10.	Administration
11.	Bunkhouse
12.	Stockade
13.	Cabins (1c through 15c)
14.	Poolhouse
15.	Pumphouse
16.	Staff House
17.	Staff House
18.	Maintenance Office
19.	Maintenance Shed
20.	Grounds Shed
21.	Carriage Shed
22.	Stable
23.	Utility Building
24.	Executive Cabin
25.	Boathouse
26.	Cabaña
27.	Sports Shed
28.	Gazebo
29.	Parking
30.	Physician Housing

Sketch of Floor Plans

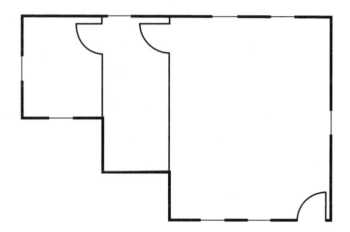

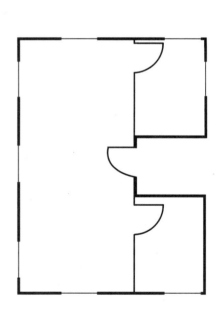

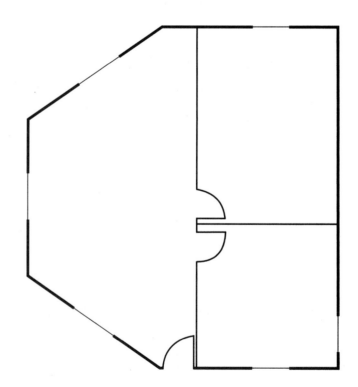

Architect's Drawing of Floor Plans

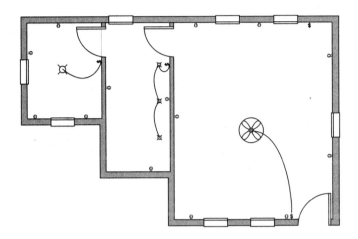

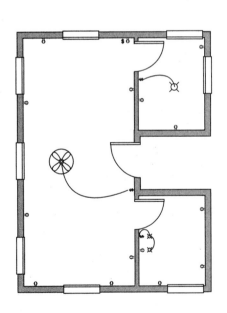

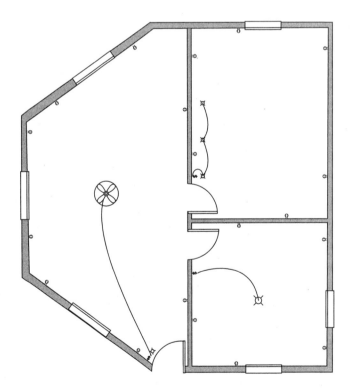

Scale: $\dfrac{1''}{8} = 1'$

Class Cabin Costs

Team	Square Footage	Cost per Cabin	Cost of 15 Cabins
1.			
2.			
3.			
4.			
5.			
6.			
7.			
8.			
9.			
10.			
11.			
12.			
13.			
14.			
15.			
16.			

Cost per Square Foot for One Cabin

Team	Cost per Cabin	Square Footage	Cost per Square Foot
1.			
2.			
3.			
4.			
5.			
6.			
7.			
8.			
9.			
10.			
11.			
12.			
13.			
14.			
15.			
16.			

ACTIVITY
2

PONDERING PERIMETER

Overview

Students design the layout for a 40-acre animal preserve to be located on the environmental camp and recognize this as a situation in architecture where increasing perimeter is desirable. Through a polyomino investigation, students determine all the perimeter possibilities for preserves made up of 40 square tiles. They develop strategies for using tiles to represent different perimeters, and analyze patterns to write relationships for finding the minimum and maximum 40-omino perimeters. Teams examine a plot plan of the campsite, decide on the location for their animal preserve and cabins, then determine the time it might take to walk their preserve perimeter.

Time. Three to four 45-minute periods.

Purpose. Students discover how perimeter can vary for a given area. They also observe how different polyominos can have the same area and the same perimeter. Students develop an understanding of the size of one acre and how to analyze data in a mathematical investigation.

Materials. *For each student:*

◆ Student Sheets 2.1–2.4

◆ Interest Link: Species Survival Plan

For each group of students:

◆ 80–100 square tiles

◆ Several sheets of $\frac{1}{4}$-inch grid paper

◆ Colored pens or pencils

◆ Calculators

◆ Customary rulers

◆ Scissors

◆ Clear tape

◆ $\frac{1}{4}$-inch transparency grid

◆ Yard stick or tape measure (optional)

For the teacher:

◆ $\frac{1}{4}$-inch transparency grid

◆ Transparencies of Student Sheets 2.1–2.4

Getting Ready

1. Gather the necessary materials and tools listed above and have them available for students.

2. Duplicate Student Sheets 2.1–2.4.

3. Prepare $\frac{1}{4}$-inch transparency grid for each group.

4. Prepare transparencies of Student Sheets 2.1–2.4.

Background Information

Throughout this activity, students develop perimeter and area concepts by exploring situations that involve fixed areas and changing perimeters. Students design the layout for a 40-acre animal preserve to be located on the environmental camp. Whereas one may be inclined to minimize perimeter for a cabin design, an animal preserve is an example of when increasing perimeter is desirable.

The design philosophy in architecture that advocates form following function is applicable to the design of animal exhibit spaces in zoos and animal preserves. Minimizing perimeter for human dwellings may reduce cost and conserve environmental resources, but an animal exhibit within a maximized perimeter may better simulate natural habitats. An amorphous shape allows for various niches suitable for animal refuge, presenting a scene whose apparent size is greater than the reality. The shape of an exhibit also influences viewing areas. A meandering perimeter can allow broader uninterrupted views and provide places to view the entire enclosure. It also creates private spaces where animals can escape from human viewing. Therefore, it is satisfying both to the animals and to the visitors.

Architectural firms involved in animal exhibit designs focus on achieving the goals of the zoo. While the health and welfare of the captive animals is their highest priority, zoo architects are also concerned with satisfying the needs of the zoo visitor and conveying the many conservation and other educational messages that the zoo delivers to millions of people. This is accomplished by focusing on the opportunities for interaction between animals and people through design exhibit techniques that range from simple observation to direct visitor participation.

Zoos and animal preserves enclose the animals for two reasons—public safety and the safety and comfort of the animals. Modern zoos have open air spaces surrounded by dry or water-filled moats and rock barriers.

Exhibition philosophy strives to accentuate the dignity of wildlife and to reveal the importance of habitat to species survival. See the Interest Link "Species Survival Plan" for further information on animal preserves.

Student Sheet 2.1 asks teams to design the shape of a 40-acre animal preserve located within the environmental camp. Students explore various shapes by joining 40 square tiles edge-to-edge to represent the 40-acre plot.

There are two measures that give important information about the size of an animal preserve—area and perimeter. In the model, the number of tiles used gives the area of the preserve, and the length of the outside edge of the connected tiles gives the perimeter of the preserve. Students work with scale to determine the length that one edge of a square tile represents. If 40 tiles represent 40 acres, then 1 tile is equivalent to 43,560 square feet. The square root of 43,560 provides the length of one edge of a square tile, approximately 209 feet. Students then identify something that has an actual length of approximately 209 feet to aid in visualizing this distance. The ability to relate this length to a familiar distance prepares students for imagining the actual size of one acre, and then 40 acres.

Through the process of designing the animal preserve, and by observing the results of other teams, students recognize how perimeter can vary for a given area. To further analyze the mathematics of this situation, Student Sheet 2.2 asks students to arrange 40 tiles in order to maximize the preserve perimeter. Students readily discover the maximum perimeter for any shape made with 40 square unit tiles is 82 linear units, and there are many designs that give the maximum perimeter.

Designs with a maximum perimeter may be in the shape of a train, an L-shape, or any other shape that meets the criterion of a minimum number of connected edges as illustrated, namely, tiles that are connected edge to edge such that four tiles never touch at the same corner.

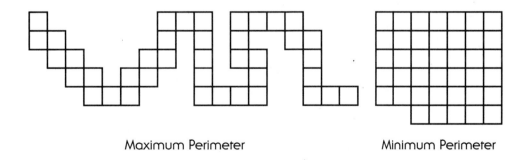

Maximum Perimeter   Minimum Perimeter

Students then explore designs that provide a minimum perimeter for 40 connected tiles and discover the minimum perimeter is 26 linear units.

Discovering that there is more than one shape that yields a maximum perimeter and more than one shape that yields a minimum perimeter leads to analyzing and comparing the various shapes with the greatest and the least perimeter. Though there are multiple polyominos that yield the maximum perimeter, there are fewer possibilities for the minimum perimeter.

For $N = 40$ tiles, the maximum perimeter $P = 2(N + 1) = 2(40 + 1) = 82$, and each variation has the minimum number of joined edges, $N - 1 = 39$. Discovering the pattern for the minimum perimeter, however, is not as straightforward. The shapes with the minimum perimeter approach that of a square. The maximum number of edges are connected in each example, which means that whenever possible, four tiles touch at the same corner.

Deciding that designs with either the minimum or maximum perimeter might be unsuitable for an animal preserve and arguing for a perimeter somewhere in between sets the stage for the next activities. Student Sheets 2.3–2.4 introduce students to polyominos and extend their investigation to explore the relationship between area and perimeter.

Shapes that are made by joining squares with whole sides touching are called *polyominos*. Any number of squares can be joined. The simplest polyomino is a domino, followed by a tromino, tetromino, pentomino, and hexomino. A polyomino formed with 40 squares is simply called a 40-omino.

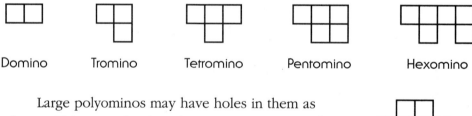

Domino   Tromino   Tetromino   Pentomino   Hexomino

Large polyominos may have holes in them as shown. This type of polyomino is not appropriate for the intended animal preserve, and therefore not included in these investigations.

Using from 1 to 40 tiles on Student Sheet 2.3, students determine all the possible polyomino perimeters for a given area. Students are involved in a mathematical investigation that systematically examines perimeters for any given number of square tiles. This is a rich investigation with numerous patterns that may emerge during group explorations and subsequent discussions.

15-omino

Polyomino perimeters are always even. Before being joined, each tile has a perimeter of four units. The combined perimeter for N individual tiles is $4 \times N$. As N increases by 1, the combined perimeter of the individual tiles is represented by the sequence of even numbers: 4, 8, 12, 16, 20, . . . , $4N$. Every time two edges are joined in a polyomino, the perimeter of the polyomino is reduced by 2 units (the connected edges) from the combined perimeter of the individual tiles, $4N$. Since an even number is always being subtracted from an even number, the resulting perimeter is always even.

Perimeter

Individual Tiles	Polyomino
$5 \times 4 = 20$ units	$20 - (5 \times 2) = 10$ units

Many students quickly see a relationship between the number of tiles N and the maximum perimeter. They determine that the maximum perimeter is twice the number of tiles plus two, or $2N + 2$. Finding a rule for determining the minimum perimeter is more complex. As polyomino data is collected, students discover several patterns that eventually lead to a method for determining the minimum perimeter. They see that the minimum perimeter can be the same for different areas; for example, areas involving 7, 8, or 9 tiles all have a minimum perimeter of 12 units. They also recognize that some perimeters, for example 14 units, can occur with a number of possible areas: 6, 7, 8, 9, 10, 11, and 12 square units.

If four squares share the same vertex, the vertex is called an *interior* point. As students continue to collect polyomino data, many will notice that there is a relationship between the number of interior points and the perimeter. In designs that represent the greatest possible perimeter, there are no interior points. For a given number of tiles, as the number of interior points increases, the perimeter decreases, as illustrated. For each interior point, the perimeter decreases by two from the maximum perimeter. All polyominos with the same area and the same number of interior points have the same perimeter. Once students realize this, it becomes a way to confirm perimeters as well as a strategy to look for additional perimeter possibilities by creating or eliminating interior points.

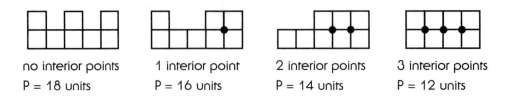

no interior points
P = 18 units

1 interior point
P = 16 units

2 interior points
P = 14 units

3 interior points
P = 12 units

Table 1 reveals some of these patterns for polyominos made with one to eight tiles. The possible perimeters are consecutive even numbers beginning with 4: 4, 6, 8, 10, 12, 14, 16, and 18. Note that for a given area, there may be more than one possible perimeter; and for a given perimeter, there may be more than one possible area.

Table 1

Polyomino Area in Square Units	Possible Perimeters in Units	Interior Points
1	4	0
2	6	0
3	8	0
4	8	1
4	10	0
5	10	1
5	12	0
6	10	2
6	12	1
6	14	0
7	12	2
7	14	1
7	16	0

Table 1 Cont'd

Polyomino Area in Square Units	Possible Perimeters in Units	Interior Points
8	12	3
8	14	2
8	16	1
8	18	0

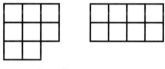

A = 8 square units
P = 12 units

In addition, students also observe that for a given area and perimeter (whether it is the minimum or not) there may be more than one polyomino, as illustrated.

Table 2 reorganizes and extends data from Table 1 to highlight polyomino areas that have a specific minimum perimeter. Note that as the perimeter increases, the number of possible areas also increases. Students analyze the patterns within these numbers.

The number of possible areas for a particular minimum perimeter is represented by consecutive pairs of repeating numbers beginning with 1. In the column depicting possible areas, notice how the square number sequence 1, 4, 9, 16, . . . and the rectangular number sequence 2, 6, 12, 20, . . . are generated by the terminating numbers of alternate rows. The terms in these sequences represent the largest area possible for a specific minimum perimeter.

Table 2

Minimum Perimeter in Units	Possible Areas in Square Units	Number of Possible Areas
4	1	1
6	2	1
8	3, 4	2
10	5, 6	2
12	7, 8, 9	3
14	10, 11, 12	3
16	13, 14, 15, 16	4
18	17, 18, 19, 20	4
20	21, 22, 23, 24, 25	5
22	26, 27, 28, 29, 30	5
24	31, 32, 33, 34, 35, 36	6
26	37, 38, 39, 40, 41, 42	6
28	43, 44, 45, 46, 47, 48, 49	7
30	50, 51, 52, 53, 54, 55, 56	7

Square Number Sequence

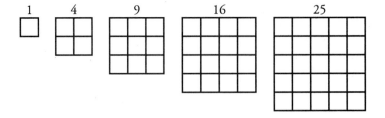

Rectangular Number Sequence

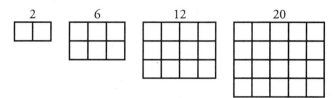

When the maximum area of a rectangle is represented by a square number, its dimensions are N by N; and when it is represented by a rectangular number, the dimensions are consecutive whole numbers, N by $N + 1$. The rectangular number dimensions, N by $N + 1$, appear in the square roots of the surrounding square numbers in the alternating sequence: $\underline{1}$, 2, $\underline{4}$, 6, $\underline{9}$, 12, $\underline{16}$, 20, $\underline{25}$ . . . . (For example: $\underline{4}$, 6, $\underline{9}$, the square root of 4 is 2; the square root of 9 is 3; the number between these two squares is 2 times 3.)

As shown below in a portion of Table 2, the number 3 represents the number of different polyomino areas with a specific minimum perimeter of 12 or 14. This number, 3, is the square root of 9, the square number that terminates the first of the two row series. In the next series, 4, the square root of 16, indicates the number of different polyomino areas with a minimum perimeter of 16 units or 18 units.

Minimum Perimeter in Units	Possible Area in Square Units	Number of Possible Areas
12	7, 8, 9	3
14	10, 11, 12	3
16	13, 14, 15, 16	4
18	17, 18, 19, 20	4

Using this information, it is possible to list all of the perimeters for any polyomino, even for very large polyominos. One way to find the possible perimeters for a 14-omino is to determine the two square numbers it is between, 9 and 16. These indicate the maximum areas for particular minimum perimeters. Recall that the perimeter P of any square is equal to four times its side length. Since the square root of the area A is equal to the side length, then $P = 4\sqrt{A}$. For an area of 9 square units, the minimum perimeter is $4\sqrt{9}$, or 12 units. For an area of 16 square units, the minimum perimeter is $4\sqrt{16}$, or 16 units. To determine the rectangular number between 9 and 16, representing the maximum area for a minimum perimeter of 14, find the product of $\sqrt{9} \times \sqrt{16}$, which equals 12. Knowing the square and rectangular numbers terminating the series of possible areas, the minimum perimeters for these terms, and the number of possible areas in each row, it is now possible to generate the missing numbers representing the possible areas for each minimum perimeter, as shown in the above table.

Students observe and generate these patterns to determine the minimum perimeter for any given number of tiles. For example, to find the minimum perimeter for an 88-omino, determine the two square numbers it is between; 88 is between 81 and 100. Both square numbers represent the maximum areas for particular minimum perimeters. The perimeter for a polyomino with an area of 81 is $4\sqrt{81}$, or 36, and the perimeter for a polyomino with an area of 100 is $4\sqrt{100}$, or 40. The number of polyomino areas with a minimum perimeter of 36 is the $\sqrt{81}$, or 9, and the number of polyomino areas with a minimum perimeter of 40 is the $\sqrt{100}$, or 10. The rectangular number between 81 and 100 is $\sqrt{81} \times \sqrt{100}$, or 90, which is the maximum area for a minimum perimeter of 38. Again, this provides enough information to generate the possible areas for these minimum perimeters. Based on this information, the minimum perimeter for a polyomino with an area of 88 square units is 38 units.

Minimum Perimeter in Units	Possible Areas in Square Units	Number of Areas
36	73, 74, 75, 76, 77, 78, 79, 80, 81	9
38	82, 83, 84, 85, 86, 87, 88, 89, 90	9
40	91, 92, 93, 94, 95, 96, 97, 98, 99, 100	10

The maximum perimeter for a polyomino with an area of 88 square units is $2N + 2$, or $2(88) + 2$, which equals 178 units. Once the minimum and the maximum perimeters are established, then the consecutive even numbers from the minimum to the maximum perimeter represent all of the possible perimeters for a given area. The possible perimeters for an 88-omino are 38, 40, 42, 44, 46, 48, 50, 52, 54, 56, . . . , 174, 176, 178, a total of 71 different perimeters, each with multiple representations. Note that as the number of tiles increases in a polyomino, the number of possible perimeters increases.

The final animal preserve design must fit within a plot for the environmental camp. Many student designs will fit within the boundaries of the plot plan on Student Sheet 2.4. Others may require minor revisions, and it is suggested teams do so without altering the perimeter. This allows students to incorporate concepts that preserve perimeter while moving squares and reconnecting edges. Besides recognizing the varied and possible 40-acre shapes with the same perimeter, they may note that disconnecting one edge of a tile or group of tiles and then reconnecting this one edge and only this one edge somewhere else on the polyomino does not affect the perimeter.

Converting the preserve perimeter from units to miles and estimating the time it will take someone to walk around each preserve provides a sense of distance. Completing the plot plan by choosing the site location for the fifteen cabins so that at least one cabin is half a mile from the lake gives experience in preparing a master plan for the client.

Presenting the Activity

Species Survival Site. Begin by having groups discuss what they know about wildlife extinction issues, animal conservation efforts, and the role zoos play in animal preservation. Supplement the discussion with information provided in the background and the Interest Link "Species Survival Plan." Orchestrate a class discussion to emphasize that saving endangered animals is one of the most important jobs of zoos today.

Distribute Student Sheet 2.1, grid paper, and square tiles to each group. Have students read the introductory statement and discuss it in their groups before explaining how teams will work as architects to propose the outline for a 40-acre species survival site within the environmental camp. Demonstrate how to connect tiles edge-to-edge and clarify what is not appropriate. (Each tile must be connected to its neighbors along one complete edge, and the shape cannot have any holes.)

While teams are working, observe interactions and initiate group discussions concerning the design features of modern zoo exhibits and animal preserves. Stress that the overriding goal of zoo design is to immerse the visitor in simulations of wild habitat in which animals can be observed behaving much as they do in nature. One aspect of this involves the actual shape of the site. Ask groups which shapes seem appropriate for an animal preserve and which do not. In these discussions, highlight the reasons for a meandering perimeter. Suggest that the final design, besides providing adequate and varied viewing areas, should also provide areas of privacy that are away from human view, as well as eliminate cross views, where visitors see other groups of visitors, in order to diminish the sense of human dominance.

Encourage discussion on how to determine the length represented by the side of one square tile. Ask them what they know about a square. Once students recognize $L = W$, they may arrive at 209 feet, using trial-and-error techniques with calculators. Support their procedures, and perhaps, have students discover the square root operation as an alternative approach.

As they finish, allow time to present and compare various designs. Display two design proposals that have different perimeters, and ask the class what they observe to be the same about both of them. Once they mention that the areas are equal, ask students to compare the perimeters. List the unit length of each perimeter, and ask students to explain how the difference occurred. Continue to list on the board the perimeter of each design. If any two are the same, stop to ask the class if they think these two designs will have the same shape, and why, or why not, before displaying them for comparison. When the list is complete, ask what patterns, if any, they notice. At this point, there may be few responses, but the question sets the stage for pattern recognition beyond the stated results. This encourages students to make predictions and analyze data as the activities progress.

Ask groups to decide if the length of the classroom is equivalent to the length one edge of a square tile represents. Listen to their reasoning before asking if the distance from the classroom to the lunchroom (or gym) would be about the same length as one edge of a square tile. Ask how one could find out. Some may suggest pacing off the distance. Proceed by having several students describe a distance they know is approximately equal in length to the edge of one square tile, and how they could confirm it.

Form Follows Function. Find out if teams think it is possible to make a shape with 40 tiles connected edge-to-edge whose perimeter is greater than those listed. Why or why not? Then ask if it might be possible to have a smaller perimeter than those listed. Why or why not? As you distribute Student Sheet 2.2, explain that by working in teams they will resolve these questions. Questions 3–5 may be completed for homework.

In the summary discussion, assess whether students sense the variety of possible perimeters for shapes using 40 tiles and the numerous shapes that exist for a particular perimeter. See if they understand the phrase *form follows function* and realize why certain shapes are or are not recommended for the animal preserve.

Polyominos. Introduce Student Sheet 2.3 as a mathematical investigation designed to provide more insight into perimeter possibilities for the animal preserve. Explain that shapes formed by joining squares edge-to-edge are referred to as *polyominos*. Mention that one strategy for finding or confirming mathematical relationships is to start with a smaller problem. Instead of analyzing the 40-ominos, the investigation begins with five tiles and systematically increases the number of tiles by one.

Distribute Student Sheet 2.3, plenty of grid paper, and the square tiles. Circulate among the groups, observing procedures and interactions. If students inquire about polyominos with holes in them, elicit discussion regarding the inappropriateness of them for the animal preserve.

After everyone has completed question 9, return to it and allow groups to present arguments indicating the possible perimeters for 26-ominos. Seize opportunities to discuss systematic methods of connecting tiles that reveal a connection between the perimeter possibilities and the number of interior points. Ask how teams plan to use their observations to continue collecting and confirming perimeter data for polyominos made with more than ten tiles. At the very least, students may propose to build, record, and verify shapes that represent the minimum perimeter before listing the other possibilities. Facilitate a closing discussion to highlight patterns and observations within their polyomino reports.

The report in question 11 on Student Sheet 2.3 is appropriate for homework.

Plot Plan. Find out if teams feel their preserve designs are appropriate for the shape of this particular environmental *campsite*. Distribute Student Sheet 2.4 along with the square tiles, and explain how the scale of the 164-acre site is equivalent to the scale on their preserve designs, that is, $\frac{1}{4}$-inch square = 1 acre. Have $\frac{1}{4}$-inch transparency grids available for groups to verify and visualize the plot plan acreage.

Once they have cut out their preserve shapes, allow teams time to experiment with placement on the plot plan before deciding if they need to rearrange squares. As they begin discussing alternatives and procedures, some teams may benefit from using the square tiles to facilitate their thinking as they move squares, maintaining the same perimeter. Others may be inclined to simply cut off squares and tape them elsewhere on the 40-acre shape until they are satisfied with the results. Have teams that redesign their preserves verify that the perimeter remains unchanged.

As teams begin calculating the actual perimeter of their preserves, stop the class and have students propose methods for finding this distance. Listen to their predictions for the time it may take to walk around the preserves. Record the distance and walking time each team offers, and then ask the class if these seem reasonable. Encourage discussion on rates of walking.

Display Transparency Master 1.6 to illustrate the plot plan for the Hole-in-the-Wall-Gang Camp. Observe team decisions on how to draw the half-mile path. Some paths may suggest a zigzag pattern, while others wind or meander toward the destination. Have students demonstrate that their finished path is approximately half a mile. Suggest each team present to the class their plot plan with preserve, path, and cabin locations in place and have them explain the reasoning used in making decisions.

Discussion Questions

1. What effect does perimeter have on the perception of space?

2. Which animals on the endangered species list could survive and thrive in your climatic region?

   a. Which animals would you recommend the zoo select?

   b. Based on your recommendations, is the 40-acre site adequate? Explain your reasoning.

3. What real-life object is about the length represented by two tiles connected in a row? By three tiles connected in a row? By four tiles connected in a row?

4. Can a polyomino have a perimeter of 9 units? Explain.

5. Name some things that have a meandering perimeter.

Assessment Questions

1. The zoo can afford the cost of developing habitat barriers for a perimeter that is 50 units in length.

   a. Use 40 tiles to design a 40-acre site with a perimeter of 50 units.

   b. Is there more than one possible enclosure with this specification? Explain your reasoning.

c. Does the specification allow for an adequate shape for an animal preserve? Explain your reasoning.

d. Making as few changes as possible, modify the design to have a perimeter of 54 units. Illustrate your design and describe the process you used to modify the design.

2. List all the possible perimeters for polyominos made with 100 square tiles, and explain how you know that you have included all possible perimeters.

3. If you know the area of a polyomino, what do you know about its perimeter?

Species Survival Plan

Zoos increase visitor awareness and appreciation for endangered wildlife. They view education as an essential component in their efforts to further wildlife conservation. Because of their commitment to captive propagation of endangered species, zoos accredited by the American Association of Zoological Parks and Aquariums (AAZPA) are the last refuge many animals have against extinction.

Many kinds of catastrophes face today's wildlife. They include human overpopulation (the human population increases by a quarter million people each day), deforestation (tropical rain forests decrease by 100 acres per minute), and air pollution. Until these global environmental threats are controlled or reversed and habitats can be saved or effectively restored, zoological facilities, national parks, and reserves will be the only sanctuaries for many of the world's endangered species.

The animal preservation and conservation movement is accelerating as fast as science can propel it. In 1981, AAZPA began the Species Survival Plan (SSP) as a cooperative venture among zoos in North America to help ensure the survival of selected wildlife species. Each SSP manages the breeding of a species in order to maintain a healthy and self-sustaining captive population. The strategies they are implementing include:

- Organizing scientifically managed captive breeding programs for selected wildlife as a hedge against extinction.
- Cooperating with other institutions and agencies to ensure integrated conservation strategies.
- Developing and implementing strategies to increase public awareness of wildlife conservation issues.
- Conducting basic and applied research to contribute to our knowledge of various species.
- Developing and testing various technologies relevant to field conservation.
- Reintroducing captive-bred wildlife into restored or secure habitat as appropriate and necessary.

Currently, 75 SSPs covering 122 individual species are located all over North America and administered by AAZPA. A species must satisfy a number of criteria to be selected for an SSP. Most are endangered or threatened in the wild and have attracted the interest of qualified professionals with time to dedicate toward their conservation. To find out more about SSPs, check out the World Wide Web site: http://www.aza.org/aza/ssp/aboutssp.html.

Species Survival Site

The camp client is donating 40 acres of the environmental camp to a major zoo to use as part of a species survival plan. The zoo will manage the site, determine the appropriate endangered species for the climate of the region, and select the numbers and types of animals best suited for the camp. Specialized staff along with the students attending the camp will oversee the day-to-day operations of the animal preserve, including observation and research.

The architect will give the client a master plan that includes the shape and location of the preserve. In planning the shape, it is important to create places for privacy, where animals can escape human view. The border should be interesting and provide varied animal refuges as well as quality viewing areas for people.

Natural barriers for confining the animals along with an observation path will be built along the perimeter that surrounds the 40 acres. Invisible interior barriers may be constructed later to separate predator species.

1. Work in teams of two within your group to create the ideal shape for an animal preserve. Prepare models using 40 square tiles to represent the 40 acres. Join the square tiles edge-to-edge, and record at least two examples per team on grid paper for consideration.

2. Wherever possible, natural barriers will be built along the perimeter of the animal preserve.
   a. Assuming each tile is 1 unit in length, calculate the perimeters of your designs.

   b. How do the perimeters compare?

Species Survival Site

3. Each square tile represents 1 acre, or 43,560 square feet.
   a. How many feet does the length of one edge of a square tile represent? Explain your reasoning.

   b. In order to visualize this distance, find something that is about the same length that one edge of a square tile represents. Describe it.

4. How might the shape of the 164-acre environmental campsite affect your design decision?

5. Select one of your animal preserve designs to present, and list the features that make it preferable to the client.

Form Follows Function

1. Use 40 square tiles to represent 40 acres. Work with a partner to design a shape that gives the greatest perimeter possible when joining squares edge-to-edge.
   a. Record the result on grid paper, and use a colored pen to highlight the perimeter.
   b. Explain how you know that your design has the greatest perimeter possible.

   c. Is this a good design for the animal preserve? Why or why not?

   d. Determine the perimeter of your design in unit lengths.

   e. If a design has the greatest perimeter possible, is it unique? Explain your reasoning.

2. Together with your partner, design a shape that has the least perimeter possible.
   a. Record the result on grid paper, and use a colored pen to highlight the perimeter.

   b. Explain how you know that your design has the least perimeter possible.

Form Follows Function

    c. Is this a good design for an animal preserve? Why or why not?

    d. Determine the perimeter of your design in unit lengths.

    e. If a design has the least perimeter possible, is it unique? Explain your reasoning.

3. How does the perimeter of the animal preserve you designed compare to the design with the greatest perimeter and the design with the least perimeter?

4. Does the shape of the animal preserve affect the cost of building it? Explain your reasoning.

5. What does the phrase *form follows function* suggest to you?

Polyomino Perimeters

Polyominos are shapes made by joining squares edge-to-edge. Work with your group to examine the possible perimeters for polyominos with a given area.

1. Use five square tiles, each with a side length of 1 unit.
   a. Rearrange the square tiles to find polyominos representing every possible perimeter. Record the shapes and their perimeters on grid paper.
   b. What is the area of each polyomino you recorded?

   c. Based on the data, what observations can you make about the perimeters?

2. Repeat the above process using one, then two, then three, and finally four square tiles.

3. Prepare a table with three columns to organize the data recorded on grid paper. Label the columns *Number of Tiles, Area (square units),* and *Possible Perimeters (units).* For each number of tiles, list the perimeters in order from least to greatest.

4. Based on these results, predict the possible perimeters for polyominos using 6 square tiles. Explain your reasoning.

5. Repeat the process from question 1 to test your perimeter predictions for 6 square tiles. Then record your findings in the table you prepared.

6. Predict possible perimeters for polyominos made with 7, 8, 9, and 10 square tiles. Then test your theories by repeating the process from question 1. Be sure to add this information to your table.

© Washington MESA Published by Dale Seymour Publications®

Polyomino Perimeters

7. At this point, what conclusions can you make about the possible perimeters for a polyomino?

8. What patterns do you notice in the table?

9. Make the following perimeter predictions for polyominos made with 26 tiles, and explain your reasoning.
   a. The longest possible perimeter.

   b. The shortest possible perimeter.

   c. Every possible perimeter.

10. Continue to make predictions with your group as you investigate the minimum, maximum, and every possible perimeter for polyominos made with 11, 12, 13, 14, 15 , . . . , 40 tiles. Be sure to verify your conclusions and record the data in the table.

11. Write a one-page report that summarizes your procedures, observations, and conclusions. Explain how an architect might use this information when developing an animal preserve.

Plot Plan

1. Examine your animal preserve design from Student Sheet 2.1.
   a. Decide on any modifications with your partner, and make them.
   b. Do you think your design will fit on the environmental camp plot plan? Explain your reasoning.

2. Using the scale $\frac{1}{4}$ inch equals the length of one square tile, draw your preserve design onto $\frac{1}{4}$-inch grid paper and cut it out.
   a. Place the 40-acre shape on the plot plan and decide its location.
   b. If your preserve does not fit on the plot plan, cut off and rearrange square acres without changing the perimeter.
   c. Once you are satisfied with the shape and location, use clear tape to secure the preserve onto the plot plan.

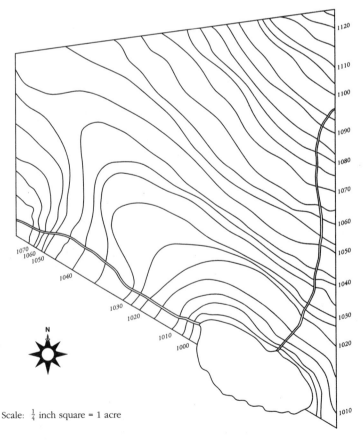

Scale: $\frac{1}{4}$ inch square = 1 acre

Plot Plan

3. Explain how you can rearrange squares on your 40-acre design without changing the perimeter.

4. There are 5,280 feet in one mile.
   a. Do you think that the preserve perimeter is more than or less than one mile? Explain your reasoning.

   b. Determine the actual perimeter of your animal preserve in miles. Show your process.

   c. Estimate the time it will take to walk around your preserve. Explain your reasoning.

5. Draw a $\frac{1}{2}$-mile path on the plot plan from the lake to the location of one cabin.

6. Mark the location of each of the remaining fourteen cabins on the plot plan with an X. Then write a short report explaining your recommendations to the client.

ACTIVITY
3

ACCENTUATING AREA

Overview

Students identify the exterior wall costs as the most expensive aspect of construction. By revisiting the polyomino investigation to consider designs for a camp guest cottage with a fixed perimeter, they explore how limiting the perimeter affects area and design. Cottage expenses are assessed, and data is graphed comparing area to cost and then area to cost per square foot. In this way, construction issues of least expensive (least total cost) versus most cost-effective (least cost per square foot) are examined. Finally, students develop strategies for finding all the possible polyomino plans with an area of 8 square units and a perimeter of 14 units to highlight cottage designs with equivalent construction costs. Through these activities, students confront the effect of shape on cost and aesthetic appeal before preparing a floor plan for a camp cottage on a limited budget.

Time. Three to four 45-minute periods.

Purpose. Students realize that the square, or a shape approaching a square, is the most efficient and cost-effective polyomino shape, yet not necessarily the best design choice in all situations.

Materials. *For each student:*

◆ Student Sheets 3.1–3.3
◆ Completed Student Sheet 2.3
◆ Calculator
◆ Customary rulers

For each group of students:

◆ Square tiles
◆ Several sheets of $\frac{1}{4}$-inch grid paper

For the teacher:

◆ Several $\frac{1}{4}$-inch transparency grids
◆ Transparencies of Student Sheets 3.1–3.3

Getting Ready

1. Have students locate completed Student Sheet 2.3.

2. Gather the necessary materials and tools listed above and have them available for students.

3. Duplicate Student Sheets 3.1–3.3.

4. Prepare transparencies of Student Sheets 3.1–3.3.

Background Information

Creating spaces for people to live and work is what architecture is all about. The architect's job can be simply stated as the manipulation of the forms, patterns, and textures within space. An architect's ability is judged by how effectively the available space is molded and structured. This does not mean everything an architect does must be totally original. The best work is often done by those who are able to combine old approaches in new and creative ways. As architects think and sketch, ideas evolve. Some are rejected and others accepted until the overall plan gains coherency and direction.

The relationship between perimeter and the area it encloses is of special importance in architecture. Perimeter defines the wall area that separates and protects us from outside elements. Wall area is available for doors, windows, and picture hanging, as well as for bookcases, entertainment systems, and other decor elements that contribute to the enjoyment of a room. However, it also represents a cost factor related to building materials, maintenance, and heating requirements. As with all other aspects of design, the architect balances conflicting concerns in the final solution.

As a result of the polyomino investigation, it becomes clear that for a given area, a building's cost-effectiveness increases as the perimeter decreases and the shape approaches or becomes a square. The exterior wall area, which includes the foundation, corresponds to the perimeter of a building and represents the most costly aspect of construction. Often the material available to construct these walls and their foundation is limited. On Student Sheet 3.1, students examine all of the possible polyomino areas with a perimeter of 14 units as potential designs for a small guest cottage. Though polyominos with the same perimeter and area may vary in shape, this activity highlights how as the area increases with a fixed perimeter, the shape approaches a square. Notice in the progression below how repositioning tiles and then adding a tile that connects to exactly two edges does not alter the perimeter.

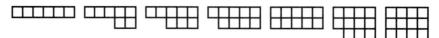

By assuming one square tile represents 36 square feet, students can calculate the actual square footage for the polyomino cottages. This in turn allows them to assess realistic cottage costs. Comparing the least expensive (least total cost) to the most cost-effective (least cost per square foot) highlights design decision dilemmas. Based on the data in the table, each added tile increases the square footage by 36 square feet and the total cost by approximately $877. From the minimum area of 6 square units to the maximum of 12 square units, the area doubles; yet the total cost of $22,290 is only about one third more than the minimum cost of $17,025.

Cottage Costs

No. of Tiles	Area (sq. ft)	Walls	Floor	Roof	Total Cost	Cost per Sq. Ft
6	216	$11,760	$2,106	$3,159	$17,025	$79
7	252	$11,760	$2,456	$3,686	$17,902	$71
8	288	$11,760	$2,808	$4,212	$18,780	$65
9	324	$11,760	$3,159	$4,738	$19,657	$61
10	360	$11,760	$3,510	$5,265	$20,535	$57
11	396	$11,760	$3,861	$5,792	$21,413	$54
12	432	$11,760	$4,212	$6,318	$22,290	$52

As the square footage increases at a constant rate, so does the total cost. Students prepare a graph illustrating this linear relationship. In the meantime, while the area is increasing, the cost per square foot is decreasing, but not at a constant rate. Because of this, the graph students make analyzing the relationship between cottage area and cost per square foot is a curve.

Student Sheet 3.2 looks at various polyomino floor plans with an area of 8 square units and a perimeter of 14 units to establish the variety of different models that have equivalent construction costs. Two polyominos are different if one cannot be reflected or rotated to coincide with the other. Each design begins with a 2-by-3 rectangle and has a total of two interior points. The remaining two tiles are systematically joined by only one edge to the polyomino in all possible ways. The twenty-one available choices shown on the next page allow the architect and client to choose a design best suited to purpose, aesthetics, and site considerations without cost variations.

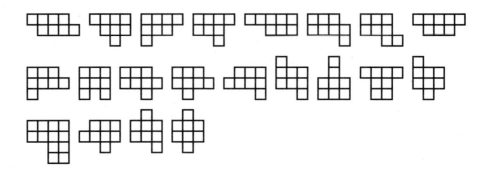

Though these models do not represent the maximum area for a polyomino with a perimeter of 14 or the minimum perimeter for an area of 8 square units, they offer more selection possibilities. When $A = 8$, there are two building designs with a minimum perimeter of 12 units. When $P = 14$, the most efficient design is a 3-by-4 rectangle with an area of 12 square units. Note that while some perimeter and area combinations can have several representations, others may have fewer or only one. The additional options provided when $A = 8$ square units and $P = 14$ units may outweigh the issue of cost effectiveness.

Polyomino Possibilities and Prices

Polyomino		Cottage			Cost
Area (sq. units)	Perimeter (units)	Area (sq. ft)	Perimeter (ft)	Total Cost	Per Sq. Ft
8	14	288	84	$18,780	$65
8	12	288	72	$17,100	$59
12	14	432	84	$22,290	$52

Designing a camp guest cottage with cost limitations on Student Sheet 3.3 gives each student a chance to apply perimeter and area concepts to architecture. Presenting potential plans within small groups and arguing the merits of each gives students the opportunity to listen, analyze, and arrive at a group recommendation. The student as architect is left to reach a compromise between what will appeal to the client, what is required, and how much money is available.

These activities promote students' awareness and perception of their surroundings and enhance their understanding of the design considerations that contribute to the quality of the structures within their environment.

Use the Technology Link "Get with the Program" and Career Link "Susan Maxman, Architect" any time during the activity to enhance student interest.

Presenting the Activity

Cottage Choices. Have students locate their data from Student Sheet 2.3 and give them time for group discussion about how an architect might use this data. Elicit their responses in a class discussion. As part of this discussion, students may recognize cost advantages to choosing the least perimeter for a given area. Ask students to identify situations where shapes with the same perimeter have different areas. After displaying several examples on the overhead, ask the class what is the most expensive part of a building. Once they identify it as the exterior wall expense, ask them to recall how and why perimeter is used to assess wall costs. End this discussion by suggesting that one way architects lower total building cost is by limiting the perimeter, which decreases the materials used for the exterior walls and foundation.

Distribute Student Sheet 3.1, grid paper, and square tiles. Circulate among groups as they work through question 1, listening to their reasoning along with their predictions. When they begin to calculate construction costs for the cottage choices, ask groups which expenses are the same for each cabin, which are different, and why.

Observe student procedures for preparing graphs representing the cost data, and take time to review scale and coordinate graphing techniques. Focus on possible scale options as well as labels for both the horizontal and vertical axes. Ask students to decide if it is necessary to use the same uniform scale on each axis, and why or why not. What happens if everyone uses a different scale? Inquire as to how one determines an appropriate scale, and how scale affects the shape and appearance of the graph.

Ask students to discuss with their groups what information they think the graph will provide. Student Sheet 3.1 may be completed for homework after students have done some initial work on it in the classroom.

After students finish the graphs, find out if they provide the information they expected. Inquire as to why one graph is linear and the other is not. Encourage their responses, concluding the discussion once they acknowledge the relationships displayed: as the area increases at a constant rate, the total cost also increases at a constant rate, presenting a linear relation; while the area increases at a constant rate, the actual cost per square foot decreases, but it is not at a constant rate, so that a curve results.

Dwelling Dilemmas. Refer once more to the polyomino investigation and remind them that groups found different shapes to represent floor plans for a particular perimeter and area. With their input, illustrate two possible 8-ominos with a perimeter of 12 units as an example. Have students hypothesize about the number of possible floor plans that might exist for a polyomino with the same area and perimeter. At this point, accept all responses, but urge them to briefly explain each theory. Revisit this question after completing Student Sheet 3.2.

Hand out Student Sheet 3.2, grid paper, and square tiles. Provide sufficient time for groups to explore question 1 and to comprehend the magnitude of the problem before asking leading questions or offering suggestions. Emphasize the importance of making sure that each recorded floor plan is indeed different. If necessary, demonstrate how two 8-ominos are the same if one can be reflected or rotated to coincide with the other.

Since each group alone may not find or agree on all the possible 8-omino floor plans with a perimeter of 14 units, initiate a class discussion to display the cumulative efforts of the class on the overhead. Have various students outline different polyominos on a transparency grid while others determine if each is unique. After a number of possibilities are determined, but before students feel the search is complete, ask groups to explain procedures for finding additional examples. As a class, decide which techniques help you know when all the possibilities are exhausted. The discussion should support more than one way to approach the problem. Suggest that students apply a method and finish the search. After all possibilities have been recorded, probe their thinking to see if they believe that all perimeter-area combinations will have this same number of floor plans.

As they resume work on Student Sheet 3.2, address individual or group concerns and ask which, if any, of the designs resemble actual buildings. Questions 2–4 may be completed for homework.

Conclude with a discussion that highlights the significance of these three situations to architecture: whether to present several design choices with equivalent costs that maintain a particular area and perimeter, or to choose a design that minimizes perimeter for the given area, or one that maximizes area for the given perimeter. Create opportunities for students to summarize the effect of shape on cost-effectiveness and, at the same time, on aesthetics and livability.

Dimension Decisions. Distribute Student Sheet 3.3, and have students read the introduction and discuss it in their groups. Suggest each student complete questions 1–7 and prepare a cottage floor plan before analyzing design proposals as a group. Point out that architects working on the same project use this technique as a way to view a variety of possibilities before reaching a final design decision. Though each draft is valued, there may be one in particular, or a combination of designs, they agree fits the situation. These questions may be completed for homework.

After groups collect information for question 8, recommend they discuss subsequent questions as a group and encourage each member to provide input. Let them know differences may show up in their reactions based on individual interpretations and preferences. Assist them in carefully analyzing design options and balancing the effects on cost, function, and appeal before making a final recommendation for the client's consideration.

Discussion Questions

1. Is the cheapest design the best design? Explain.

2. How can a square tile represent 43,560 square feet in a previous activity and 36 square feet in this activity?

3. What do you know about the area of a shape when the perimeter is given?

Assessment Questions

1. Determine if the following statements are true or false. Explain your reasoning.

    a. Two different polyominos can have the same perimeter and area.

    b. Two different polyominos can have the same perimeter, yet have different areas.

    c. Two different polyominos can have the same area, yet have different perimeters.

2. Use the square tiles to design the camp director's dwelling with an area of 12 square units and a perimeter of 20 units. Record your layout on grid paper.

    a. What is the minimum perimeter for a 12-omino? Explain your reasoning.

    b. What is the maximum area for a polyomino with a perimeter of 20 units? Explain your reasoning.

c. Using the scale 1 square tile = 50 square feet, determine the actual dwelling measurements and estimate construction costs without including interior wall expenses. Complete the table below for each design.

Dwelling Data

Polyomino		Director's Dwelling		Construction Costs	
Area (sq. units)	Perimeter (units)	Area (sq. ft)	Perimeter (ft)	Total	Per Sq. Ft
12	20				
12	Minimum				
Maximum	20				

d. Choose one of these design proposals for the camp, and explain your recommendation.

3. Why would an architect need to know about perimeter and area relationships?

Get with the Program

Architectural design begins with simple sketches or doodles on tracing paper, and progresses through increasing levels of detail to the working drawings from which a structure is built. Computer-aided design systems can facilitate all but the earliest steps of this process. New software and improved graphics-rendering techniques allow architects to work through the entire preliminary design process—sketching and exploring alternative designs, refining these, and viewing realistic images of them generated in three dimensions. These programs relieve designers of labor-intensive drawing and provide more freedom to explore new ideas. As a result, the computer contributes to the creative side of architecture.

Architect Using CAD Program

Sophisticated computer graphics programs produce images much more useful to architects and clients than the drawings and painstakingly constructed small-scale physical models traditionally used. Whereas models only give the architect and client a birds-eye view of the building or interior, computer graphics are capable of showing how the finished design will actually work. These programs can display images of the building from different perspectives in rapid succession, capturing subtle changes of light and shadow, and give the client a better sense of what it will be like to walk through the building after it has been constructed. Because of the extraordinary advances in software and hardware, architects are able to see the effects of their design decisions immediately and to revise them quickly.

Although the initial rough sketches for a design may always be done on the backs of napkins, the coming decade will see computer programs that are simple to learn and to use, yet powerful enough to handle the design of entire buildings down to the smallest detail and capable of generating moving photo-realistic images.

Susan Maxman, Architect

Susan Maxman is an architect of extraordinary accomplishments by any measure. But her awards and titles are even more remarkable considering she began her architecture training at the age of 36 while raising six children. Her rise to prominence in the profession can be explained by her convictions that one should pursue one's dreams, and, in the words of her father, "There is no such word as *can't*."

When Susan first considered studying architecture in the late 1950s, the profession was virtually all male. But Susan believes that soon gender will cease to be an issue in the practice of architecture. Already, women and men are entering schools of architecture in roughly equal numbers, and the current generation of graduates are accustomed to having women as professional peers.

Today, as the director of her own firm of thirteen architects in Philadelphia, Ms. Maxman focuses on environmentally sensitive projects for non-profit, community-based groups. Her firm practices environmentally responsible architecture by designing buildings that fit into their surroundings, use local building materials, are sensitive to user needs, and are in harmony with the community. She believes architects need to solve problems for their clients rather than to create showy buildings.

Through sustainable design, Susan realized that she could do something to reduce the damaging effects that construction has on the environment. A sustainable design philosophy emphasizes quality of life, cost-effectiveness, and a concern for the future. A sustainable design means refusing to use materials that cannot be easily replaced, such as hard woods from old-growth forests. For Susan, this means "unless grown and harvested selectively to meet sustainable criteria, I can't use cedar, and it's my absolute favorite." Sustainable designs also require limiting consumption as much as possible. "Buildings, you see, use one third of this country's energy." Her firm uses computer models to ensure maximum energy efficiency.

One of her award-winning designs is Camp Tweedale, a four-cabin complex plus an activity lodge for the Freedom Valley Girl Scout Council. The goal was to provide winterized cabin structures while maintaining a sense of outdoor camping year round. With that in mind, the buildings are designed to provide another dimension to the campers' experience and not upstage the natural setting.

The buildings are positioned on the site to not disturb its distinct natural features, which include a small and mostly level open area surrounded by steep wooded slopes. The cabins are nestled at the edge of the woods with rear decks that cantilever over the slopes below. All the structures are constructed with materials that are appropriately rustic and durable. Because of the success of this project, the firms expertise is in high demand for projects in natural settings.

Her firm is now in the process of designing an Environmental Visitors Center for the U.S. Fish and Wildlife's natural habitat preserve on a marsh near downtown Philadelphia. They are also actively involved in an urban demonstration project to design affordable and attractive housing for the inner city. Susan meets with neighborhood groups and listens to their ideas, always keeping her designs within the parameters of what the client needs.

Susan is the first and only woman elected to the office of president in the 135-year history of the American Institute of Architects. Her 1993 term as president was dedicated to emphasizing the architect's role in helping to save the environment. Susan believes we are too willing to throw away pristine landscapes while incorporating them into the suburban sprawl. As a society, we often build whenever and wherever we please, developing more and more of our lands. This is an issue architects need to address.

Camp Tweedale Activity Building
Lower Oxford Township, Pennsylvania
Susan Maxman Architects

Because how and where we build are often determined by the plans of architects, they are trained to look at the big picture, to create a balance between the varying needs of society and those of nature. Susan wonders if we should retain the right to develop our land with few restrictions, or if it would be more fitting for us to adopt the Native American belief, "We do not inherit our land from our ancestors, we borrow it from future generations."

Cottage Choices

The master plan for the camp includes small guest cottages to be used by visiting zoo personnel or environmental instructors. Each cabin will accommodate one or two people. Because perimeter influences cost, the client has asked that the architects investigate various floor plans for a guest cottage that has a specific perimeter.

1. Use square tiles along with the table you prepared for Student Sheet 2.3 to design polyomino cottages that have a perimeter of 14 units and different areas.

   a. Draw a floor plan on grid paper to represent every possible polyomino area with a perimeter equivalent to 14 units. List the possible areas.

   b. Is there more than one design for each possible area representation with this perimeter? Explain.

   c. Which floor plan do you prefer? Explain the reasons for your preference.

   d. Based on your designs, predict which cottage is the least expensive to build and explain your reasoning.

   e. Predict which of your designs is the most cost-effective to build, and explain your reasoning.

Cottage Choices

2. Let the length of one tile equal 6 feet.
   a. Determine the number of square feet that a tile represents, and explain your reasoning.

   b. Use this scale to calculate and record the actual square footage for each cottage floor plan drawn in question 1a.

Number of Tiles						
Square Feet						

3. The interior wall expense has a minor influence on construction costs, and it is often excluded from initial estimates. Without considering interior wall expenses, use the price estimates below to calculate costs for each cottage area. Use your data to complete the table on the next page and calculate the cost per square foot for each cottage area. Round costs to the nearest dollar.

Expense Estimates

Floors	$9.75	per square foot
10-Foot-High Exterior Walls	$140.00	per linear foot
Roof	1.5	times the floor cost

Cottage Choices

Cottage Costs

Cottage Area (sq. ft)	Walls	Floor	Roof	Total Cost	Cost per Sq. Ft

4. Using the data from your table on cottage costs:
   a. Prepare a graph comparing area to total cost. Describe the shape of the graph and the relationship it shows between area and total cost.

   b. Prepare a second graph comparing area to cost per square foot. Describe the shape of the graph and the relationship it shows between area and cost per square foot.

Cottage Choices

5. What do the graphs and the table show about the relationship between area, total cost, and cost per square foot?

6. Describe the best polyomino shape for a cottage design with a perimeter of 14 tile units, and explain your reasoning.

Design Dilemmas

1. Use the square tiles to design various polyomino floor plans for cottages with an area of 8 square units that have a perimeter of 14 units.

   a. Sketch on grid paper several of these designs, making sure that each one is different from the others.

   b. How many different floor plans are there that fit this description? Explain your procedures for determining this.

   c. What do you know about the cost of building each of these cottages? Explain your reasoning.

   d. Which design do you prefer? Why? Is it livable?

2. a. What is the most cost-effective perimeter for a polyomino with an area of 8 square units? Explain your reasoning.

   b. Sketch different polyomino floor plans on grid paper for 8-square-unit cottages that have the least perimeter.

   c. How many different building plans exist with these specifications? Explain your reasoning.

   d. Which of these designs do you prefer? Why?

   e. How do the costs to build these cottages compare with those in question 1?

Design Dilemmas

3. a. What is the most cost-effective area for a polyomino with a perimeter of 14 units? Explain your reasoning.

   b. How many different cottage plans exist with these specifications? Explain your reasoning.

   c. Compare the construction costs with those for the cottages in questions 1 and 2.

4. State several reasons why an architect might be interested in the information developed in questions 1, 2, and 3.

Dimension Decisions

The client plans to build three guest cottages on the campsite and insists the total expenses not exceed $20,000 per cottage. Design a two-bedroom cottage for the client that includes a sitting room and one bathroom with a shower, sink, and toilet.

Expense Estimates

Floors	$9.75	per square foot
10-Foot-High Exterior walls	$140.00	per linear foot
10-Foot-High Interior Walls	$35.00	per linear foot
Roof	1.5	times the floor cost

1. Begin with a series of flow diagrams to brainstorm ideas.

2. Let $\frac{1}{4}$ inch = 1 foot. Prepare a cottage floor plan on grid paper and label all the dimensions.
   a. Using the above expense estimates, list the itemized expenses and verify that the total cost is within the $20,000 limit.

Dimension Decisions

b. Describe the shape of your cottage design. Explain why you selected this shape.

c. Indicate the placement of doors, windows, interior walls, furniture, and bathroom facilities on the floor plan.

3. Calculate the square footage of your cottage design.

4. Find the cost per square foot to build your cottage.

5. Based on your calculations, the camp client will be charged approximately $ _____ for the materials necessary to build one cottage and $ _____ for a total of three camp cottages.

Dimension Decisions

6. List several reasons why your cottage should be selected and recommended to the camp client.

7. Compare cottage designs and costs within your group.

Cottage Construction Costs

Name	Square Footage	Exterior Wall Expense	1 Cottage	3 Cottages	Cost per Sq. Ft
1.					
2.					
3.					
4.					

   a. Which designs serve the intended purpose? Explain.

   b. Which designs are the most appealing to you? Why?

Dimension Decisions

    c. Which designs are the most cost-effective? Explain your reasoning.

    d. Which designs do you think will appeal to the client? Why?

    e. Which designs do you think will appeal to the guests? Why?

8. From the above cottage choices, select one your group will recommend to the camp client. Explain the basis for your choice.

ACTIVITY
4

MODIFICATIONS AND MODELS

Overview

Students collaborate in groups of four to revise preliminary camp cabin designs from Activity 1 and prepare a final plan that incorporates the needs of the client as well as area and perimeter relationships developed in previous activities. Each group follows steps to build a cardstock model of their cabin to assess the visual effects. They compile construction costs and write a short report detailing their cabin's features.

Time. Three to four 50-minute periods.

Purpose. Students develop an appreciation of the design process that takes the architectural team through a series of revisions toward the final solution and presentation model.

Materials. *For each student:*

◆ Student Sheets 4.1–4.2

For each group of students:

◆ Cabin floor plans from Activity 1
◆ Calculators
◆ Several sheets of $\frac{1}{4}$-inch grid paper
◆ Customary rulers
◆ 4–6 sheets of $8\frac{1}{2}$-inch by 11-inch cardstock
◆ Clear tape
◆ Scissors
◆ X-Acto® knife (optional)
◆ 9-inch by 12-inch manila envelopes (optional)

For the teacher:

◆ Transparencies of Student Sheets 4.1–4.2
◆ List of student responses from Activity 1 on the role of mathematics in architecture

Getting Ready

1. Gather the necessary materials and tools listed above and have them available for the students.

2. Locate initial student responses from Activity 1 on the role of mathematics in architecture.

3. Have students locate their preliminary cabin floor plans from Activity 1.

4. Prepare a place in the classroom for storing and displaying the cabin models.

5. Duplicate Student Sheets 4.1–4.2.

6. Prepare transparencies of Student Sheets 4.1–4.2.

Background Information

The practice of architecture includes defining problems, evaluating alternatives, and implementing solutions. The development of an architectural design follows a standard process. After bringing together ideas and preparing the initial floor plan, architects gather more information, generate new ideas, and determine the effectiveness of various design proposals. Each completed design gives new insights into the problem. Based on a cycle of design and feedback, architects derive the best possible plan and create a presentation model in addition to drawings for the client's approval.

In this activity, students work in groups of four on Student Sheet 4.1, refining their original camp cabin designs to reflect concepts and ideas developed in this module. Their final floor plan may be a further refinement of an initial design, incorporate the best aspects of previous plans, or be completely different from prior attempts. The decision-making process groups use on Student Sheets 4.1–4.2 to arrive at design consensus is an important aspect of the final architectural product.

Architectural plans include both a floor plan and a series of drawings that illustrate the exterior view from each side of the building, called *elevations*. They show the height and length of each exterior wall, as well as the door and window placements. Both floor plans and elevations are used to build models. On Student Sheet 4.2, students make plans for the walls of their cabins, part of an elevation. Directions are provided for building cardstock models based on their completed floor plans and elevation drawings. Sometimes design problems become apparent when architects move from a two-dimensional drawing to a three-dimensional model. At the same time, solutions become easier to see. Architects refine the model to make the design work better, then change the drawings to match.

Building code requirements influence design. If a home or cabin is gas-heated, window space cannot exceed 25 percent of the floor area. Because of the increased heating costs, when using electric heat, window area must be within 15 percent of the floor area. In practice, there are a number of modifiers to this based on insulation and window types. With this in mind, students restrict window area on their models to within 25 percent of the floor area.

Arrange a place to store the models in progress and to display them when finished. Large manila envelopes can hold pieces temporarily.

Use the History Link "The Cambridge School" and the Writing Link "Architect Anecdotes" any time during the activity to enhance student interest.

Presenting the Activity

Final Floor. Reexamine and continue the list of student responses from Activity 1 on the role of mathematics in architecture. As more details are added, point out the increased level of their collective understanding now that they have had several design opportunities. Suggest that this phenomenon of developing greater understanding as the result of experience occurs for architects within the challenges of each project. In any design process there is a recurring cycle of design and feedback that takes the architect through a series of revisions toward the final solution and presentation model.

Distribute Student Sheet 4.1 and grid paper. Ask students to collaborate with their group in order to incorporate their design experiences and insights into developing a final floor plan for the camp cabin that satisfies the specifications as to function as well as appeals to the financial and aesthetic needs of the client.

Circulate among the groups to promote discussion and listening. Suggest that the solutions architects come up with first may not necessarily be the best ones. Encourage individuals to contribute by suggesting their thoughts may inspire other ideas or connect to something someone else has in mind. As they struggle to find a way to reach consensus, have students refocus and decide what needs to be resolved.

Team Tasks. Once a group has formulated their final floor plan, distribute Student Sheet 4.2 along with grid paper, calculators, cardstock, rulers, tape, and scissors. Ask why architects make scale models of the buildings they design. Continue the discussion, allowing them to consider how the model is used to assess the visual effects that are not apparent from the floor plan. Explain that they will design and complete roofs for the cabin models in the next activity.

Support group efforts to allocate the tasks, recognizing that some things are clearly dependent upon others. Suggest they focus on what individuals can accomplish while team members are finalizing the floor plan: taping wall strips together, estimating costs, or listing reasons why the client should choose their design.

Observe their process for constructing cabin walls as well as determining window and door locations. Give input as necessary, and ask them how high up on the walls the windows should be placed. Have teams convince you that the amount of window area in their models does not exceed 25 percent of the floor area. Inquire as to what 25 percent means and how they might apply this information. Find out if they think this is a good requirement, and why or why not.

It is possible that initial ideas on window or door placement may need revision once the walls surround the base. Some may find their three-dimensional view does not resemble what they envisioned in two dimensions. Assure them this is common, and allow time for teams to reassess the situation before cutting out windows and doors. (Some teams may prefer pasting on windows to cutting them out). Be sure to clarify where and how to store the models. Remind teams to put their names on the base of the completed model for quick identification.

Set a reasonable completion date and time allotment to work on this project in class, realizing that some class time will be used to explore roof possibilities in the next activity before the models and reports can be completed.

Discussion Questions

1. How does your group's final floor plan compare in size and shape to your initial designs from Activity 1?

2. Which are more appealing, the initial designs or the final revisions? Explain.

3. Which serve the purpose better, the initial designs or the final revisions? Explain.

Assessment Questions

1. This is a preliminary floor plan for a camp cabin. The architect wants to decrease perimeter costs in her revision while maintaining the area.

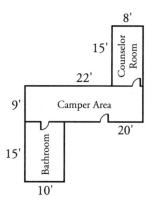

   a. What suggestions can you make?

   b. Revise the floor plan to match your suggestions.

   c. How does your revision affect construction costs?

2. The architect now wants a revision that maintains the initial perimeter costs, but increases the cabin's area.

   a. What suggestions can you make?

   b. Revise the floor plan to match your suggestions.

   c. How does your revision affect construction costs?

3. The architect wants to present the client with an alternate plan that maintains both the perimeter and area of her original design.

   a. What suggestions can you make?

   b. Revise the floor plan to match your suggestions.

   c. How does your revision affect construction costs?

The Cambridge School

The Cambridge School of Architecture was founded for the education of women in 1915. It began with one woman's request for tutoring in architectural drafting from an instructor at the Harvard School of Architecture, which did not allow women to attend. It was not long before other women requested such instruction, and the continued interest of women seeking instruction in architecture set the foundation for the first recognized architectural school for women in the United States.

The curriculum was based upon the firm conviction of the time that women were only suited for domestic architecture—the design and construction of houses. Though this may have been the objective of the school, it was not the goal of the six women who prevailed upon the liberal ideals of the two founding instructors, Henry Frost and Bremer Pond. These women had come to learn everything they could, and they soon stretched the boundaries of the domestic realm to include schools, hospitals, pavilions, concert halls, country estates, restaurants, modern art centers, and even the planning and designing of entire villages. However, it was not until 1941 that Henry Frost could publicly admit the fact that the Cambridge School students were not being taught solely domestic architecture.

The three-and-a-half-year course of study had three major divisions—design, construction, and freehand drawing. Students were required to take and demonstrate proficiency in such courses as architectural and landscape design, working drawings for construction purposes, history, plant materials, mathematics, graphics, and sketching. The school realized that architecture and landscape architecture are professions combining requirements of design, technical understanding, and business sense. Collaboration and cooperation among these related disciplines were practiced throughout the school's existence. This interdisciplinary educational notion was not recognized at other schools. Only much later, in the 1940s, did Harvard stress the relationship between architecture and landscape architecture.

The Cambridge School was established not to teach architecture to women in the passive manner or as only an intellectual pursuit, but to ensure that they could actively practice their profession upon graduation. In 1930, 83 percent of the graduates were active in professional work. Though such achievements were in some respects remarkable, they certainly do not indicate that obtaining work

"Evening Work"
Students at the Cambridge
School of Architecture

was easy for these women. For one thing, the doubts and prejudices of society affected the type of work available to women.

Because it only had the authority to grant certificates to its graduates, in 1932 the Cambridge School became part of Smith College in order to grant official degrees in architecture. Unhappily, ten years later the school closed.

The Cambridge School of Architecture was killed by unbalanced budgets, changing times, and the need of Harvard's architectural school to fill its ranks, which were being depleted by the war effort.

Though the Cambridge School closed, its enthusiastic students continued their education at Harvard with the extremely large registration of twenty-eight women in 1942. Though the founders and many of the alumnae felt the closing of the Cambridge School was a tragedy, they were optimistic that this consolidation was a natural step. Sadly, within ten years, the enrollment of women was cut in half.

Women were indeed being admitted to universities and, at least at Harvard, there were few policies of discrimination. But where are the women architects who continue the traditions of the Cambridge School women? There are relatively few women architects practicing in this country today or studying in its professional schools. Of the 56,000 current members of the American Institute of Architects, only about 6,000 are women. The end of the Cambridge School marked the end of an era. The idea of a school of architecture solely for women was not the aim of the Cambridge School; but the School's goal of encouraging women in architecture is still an issue and a dream that has not been fulfilled.

Architect Anecdotes

When the architects at Hammond Beeby and Babka were hired to develop the Hole-in-the-Wall Gang Camp, they knew they had less than eighteen months to design and complete a project for which only the mission was known: to provide a full outdoor experience for those who would normally be denied that possibility by the nature of their physical needs. This was a very intense timeline, since there were no other camp projects quite like this in existence. This meant the architects had to devise their own program for the camp and invent new types of buildings to accomplish the goals. The principal architects went to work, visualizing a western town theme. They determined the camp would need thirty-five different buildings, including fifteen log cabins.

At this point, they parceled out the work to several design teams within their office. Each team was given three buildings to design. For instance, one design team was responsible for the cabin prototype, the administration building, and the twin towers. Because of the timeline, they worked separately on their team projects, hoping that the final designs would all work aesthetically when put together. Everyone built models of their specific buildings and was relieved at how well they fit together and complemented the site. Some of the initial models were eventually modified, and others were never built.

The architects wanted the sleeping areas to be authentic log cabins, reflecting the rustic element the client was seeking. They found and hired a contractor who specialized in building log cabins. Logs tend to shrink quite a bit after construction, which can be a tricky proposition for an inexperienced builder. Part of the problem is that the doors and windows along with their casings are made out of lumber that has far less shrinkage than logs. What do you think would happen to the cabin if the architects did not know this?

One day several of the architects flew to Canada, expecting to see a completed model of their proposed Canadian red pine cabin. They arrived to see only four logs in place! Can you imagine how they felt? The contractor was replaced. Since there were fifteen cabins, the new contractor, who had little previous experience building log cabins, and his crew gained experience as each one was built. The first two were not as well done as the later ones, but the project was completed on time!

Even though its foundation was in place, the lookout tower was not constructed. The fire marshal would not allow it to be built when he realized the design did not include two separate ways to get down.

After the first year of operation, everyone agreed a theater was the only thing missing. Again a team of architects went to work and designed a theater building that fit into the western theme. In order to disguise the acoustical ceiling, they covered it with a starburst pattern of 200 copper stars. Each one was hand screwed into the ceiling by the lead architect himself!

Write an anecdote reflecting something that happened while you were designing or building a model for the proposed environmental camp in this module.

Final Floor

Work in teams of four to create the optimal camp cabin floor plan, including door and window placements. Just as an architectural team would do, you will need to make compromises to come to an acceptable solution. Use the following guidelines to develop a workable plan.

1. Recall the facts about the site and building specifications.
    a. Review the site and building specifications.
    b. Clearly state the purpose of the camp cabin.
    c. Discuss what the client wants.

2. Brainstorm solutions.
    a. Give everyone a chance to suggest ideas.

    b. Have someone write the ideas down on paper.

    c. Do not judge or eliminate any ideas during this session.

3. Make a decision. Look closely at the solutions you have, and as a group, pick the one that works best.

Final Floor

4. Examine the decision.
   a. How does the idea match the cabin criteria?

   b. How will it appeal to the client?

   c. Will it have financial appeal?

   d. How will it appeal to the campers?

   e. How will it appeal to the counselors?

   f. How does it appeal to you aesthetically?

5. Were you able to give satisfactory answers to the questions in number 4? If so, you probably have a creative and workable solution to the problem. If not, return to question 3, generate new ideas, and revise your plan.

6. Now that your group has come up with the best possible solution, you can look forward to making your idea become reality.

Team Tasks

Below are four team tasks your group needs to complete. Divide the tasks, making sure that two or more people are responsible for each one. Keep in mind that all tasks may be in progress at the same time. For example, while the floor plan is being finalized, wall strips can be taped together for the model, and the report can be started.

1. Finalize the floor plan.
    a. Let $\frac{1}{4}$ inch = 1 foot. Draw the cabin floor plan on grid paper. Indicate the dimensions along the perimeter, and show the location of doorways, windows, furniture, and bathroom facilities.

    b. Determine the square footage of the cabin and explain your procedures.

2. Determine costs.
    a. Use the estimates to approximate the total cost for building the cabin.

Expense Estimates

Floors	$9.75	per square foot
10-Foot-High Exterior Walls	$140.00	per linear foot
10-Foot-High Interior Walls	$35.00	per linear foot
Roof	1.5	times the floor cost

   b. The camp client will be charged approximately $ _____ to build one cabin and $ _____ for fifteen camp cabins.

   c. Calculate the cost per square foot for the cabin design.

3. Build a model.
   a. Let $\frac{1}{4}$ inch = 1 foot. Accurately cut out a cardstock base for the cabin that duplicates the final floor plan. Transfer all interior wall, window, and door markings.
   b. Cut several strips of cardstock to represent 10-foot-high walls. Tape them together to form one long, continuous strip. Crease the wall strip at appropriate lengths to surround the base. Draw onto the wall strip the location of windows and doors.
   c. Buildings must comply with codes and restrictions. These ensure the finished product will be structurally sound and energy-efficient. One restriction states that the total window area cannot exceed 25 percent of the floor area. Determine if the total window area is less than 25 percent of the floor area. Show your process and explain your reasoning. If necessary, change window sizes and locations until your model meets code.

   d. Surround the base with the walls, without permanently attaching them, to assess your design.
   e. Carefully cut out the windows. Cut out three sides on each door, leaving the side that has the hinge intact.
   f. Tape the wall strip along the cabin base and tape the ends together.
   g. Build interior walls with doorways, taping them to the base as well.

4. Prepare a short report to present with your model that addresses cost issues, describes any special features, and gives reasons why the client should choose your cabin design.

ACTIVITY
5

RAISING
THE ROOF

Overview

After investigating roof pitch and its effect on aesthetics, cost, and function, students select a suitable pitch for their cabin model and follow instructions to construct a simple gable roof. Groups consider at least one other roof design appropriate for their cabin from the options provided before finalizing their presentation model.

Time. Three to four 50-minute periods.

Purpose. Students understand the mathematics of pitch and span as it relates to roof design and recognize the effect different roof styles have on the appearance of a building.

Materials. *For each student:*

◆ Student Sheets 5.1–5.3

For each group of students:

◆ Calculators

◆ Several sheets of grid paper

◆ Customary rulers

◆ Sheets of $8\frac{1}{2}$-inch by 11-inch cardstock

◆ Clear tape

◆ Scissors

◆ Protractors or Cuisenaire® angle rulers

For the teacher:

◆ Transparency Master 5.4

◆ Transparencies of Student Sheets 5.1–5.3

Getting Ready

1. Gather the necessary materials and tools listed above and have them available for students.

2. Duplicate Student Sheets 5.1–5.3.

3. Prepare Transparency Master 5.4 and transparencies of Student Sheets 5.1–5.3.

Background Information

Architects develop the roof design in conjunction with the building plans. A roof protects and decorates a building, as well as provides a sense of resolution. It can influence the aesthetic effect, mask or enhance the building's purpose, and be a dominating or passive feature. Steeply pitched roofs imply a climate with heavy snowfalls; the flat roofs of hotter regions spread out beyond the walls to give shade. Often more than one roof design is appropriate for a structure, though each may serve a different purpose.

When the perimeter of a building is complicated, architects may choose a flat roof. A flat roof is not always a good solution, however. It works in some climates and is certainly cost-effective, but a flat roof is maintenance intensive and not recommended where snowfall is a factor.

For the camp cabin, a standing seam metal roof with a two-foot overhang will be used, and the interior rafters will be visible to the campers. The rafters are sized and spaced to support the weight of the roof itself plus any snow that can be expected.

A standing seam metal roof is made of two-foot wide strips of metal joined together by folding the edges together and over, similar to how one folds aluminum foil around food to keep it airtight. The securely folded seams prevent water from leaking through the roof. The result is a series of wide, raised standing seams along the roof panel.

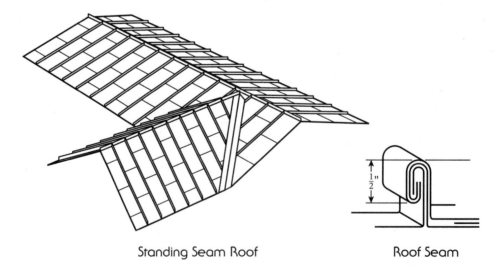

Standing Seam Roof   Roof Seam

Besides being lightweight, fireproof, and durable, metal roofing has strong architectural appeal. It is relatively easy and quick to install, as well as readily available in many colors, textures, and profiles. Standing seam metal roofs are particularly common in rural areas or where the ability to shed snow is important. They may also be required roofing in heavily timbered areas.

Guidelines are provided for four simple roof styles appropriate for the camp cabins. The gable, gable with non-centered ridge, shed, and intersecting roof designs displayed on Transparency Master 5.4 can all be adapted for nonrectangular floor plans. After completing a gable roof for their model, groups are asked to construct at least one other type of roof before choosing the design that seems most appropriate for their cabin model.

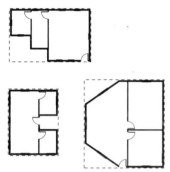

A simple gable roof can be designed for each cabin by outlining a best-fit rectangle around a nonrectangular shape. This results in various-sized overhangs along the perimeter that provide sheltered outdoor areas for porches, patios, or storage. Depending on the overhang, pillars may be required for support, and any gaps between the walls and the roof must be enclosed. While it is not the most economical roof, a gable roof does provide usable, covered outdoor space that may balance additional expenses. The examples show best-fit rectangles for floor plans displayed on Transparency Master 1.7.

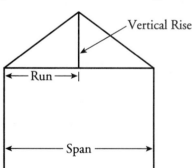

The width of the building is called the *span,* which represents the base of the triangles on a gable roof. The *vertical rise* is the perpendicular distance from the ridge to the base of the gable. It divides the gable into two congruent right triangles. The base of each right triangle is half the span and designates the *run*.

The run is an important dimension to the architect and builder. They consider the pitch of a roof to be the ratio *rise:run*. Technically, the pitch can be anything the designer wants, but the most common pitches are 1:1, 1:2, and 1:3.

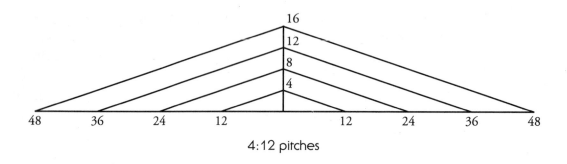

16
12
8
4

48   36   24   12   12   24   36   48

4:12 pitches

Architects and builders are interested in the rise per foot of a roof. The conventional method is to state the pitch ratio relative to 12 inches. For example, they refer to a 1:2 pitch as 6:12 or a 1:3 pitch as 4:12. A 4:12 pitch means the vertical rise increases 4 inches every time an additional foot is added to the run.

Potential weather conditions influence the type of roofing material used as well as acceptable building spans and roof pitches. When snow is a possibility, architects may consider a pitch less than 1:3 unacceptable for weight bearing and runoff purposes. If it is a standing seam metal roof, then a pitch of 1:4 is acceptable.

Pitch and span work together to create an aesthetically balanced appearance in the completed structure. If the desired pitch and span for a particular gable roof are known, the vertical rise can be determined using equivalencies. If the camp cabin has a span of 36 feet, then it has a run of 18 feet, and for a 1:1 pitch, the vertical height is 18 feet.

For any roof span, the steeper the pitch, the taller the roof from base to ridge. When this height exceeds the building's height, the total volume of the roof is excessive for a one-story building and may look overwhelming and out of proportion. This suggests a maximum vertical rise of 10 feet for a cabin with 10-foot walls. On many cabin designs, a 1:1 pitch will be aesthetically pleasing; but as the span increases, so does the vertical rise for a given pitch. Simply lowering the pitch to 1:2 or 1:3 may alleviate this problem. For example, a roof with a 36-foot span, using a 1:2 pitch gives a 9-foot vertical rise, which architects consider more aesthetically acceptable.

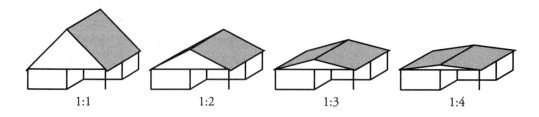

1:1   1:2   1:3   1:4

A narrow roof span allows for a steeper roof without compromising appearance. If the building span is 16 feet, than the vertical rise with a 1:1 pitch is only 8 feet. If the span is 24 feet, then the vertical rise with a 1:1 pitch is now 12 feet; whereas a 1:2 pitch would be 6 feet. The gables are always erected on the narrowest sides of the building to allow for a steeper pitch.

As the roof pitch on a particular cabin base increases, the roof panel and gable areas also increase, which influences the cost of construction materials. Therefore, it is cost-effective to choose the minimum pitch necessary to satisfy load and weight-bearing conditions while maintaining aesthetic appeal. Just as too high a vertical rise may be unappealing, so may be too low a vertical rise. Once students select a roof pitch on Student Sheet 5.1, they construct a simple gable roof for their cabin models. First, they outline a rectangle of best-fit that encloses their cabin floor plan, and then they follow the instructions on Student Sheet 5.2.

Students compute the actual width of the roof panels and rafter lengths using scaling techniques based on measurements taken from their models. Architects and builders apply the Pythagorean theorem to determine these dimensions. Since the gable represents two congruent right triangles, the run constitutes one leg and the vertical rise the other leg. The width of the roof panel corresponds to the hypotenuse of this right triangle. If a and b represent the legs and c the hypotenuse, solving the equation $a^2 + b^2 = c^2$ for c, and then adding two feet for the overhang provides the desired information. Students familiar with right triangle properties may recognize and use this method.

The 2-foot overhang represents the length the roof panel extends beyond the exterior walls and the gables. Students outline the rectangle of best fit on their floor plan with a 2-foot border to visualize and approximate the roof line, as well as to determine gable and roof panel measurements. When they complete their roofs, students can measure the distance the roof edge is from the wall on their models and use scale techniques to determine the actual distance. Though the overhang distance from the walls on the gable ends is 2 feet, the actual distance the bottom edge of the roof panel is from the side walls will always be less than 2 feet. This distance from the wall varies inversely with the pitch of the roof; that is, the steeper the roof, the closer the 2-foot overhang will be to the wall.

The overhang distance from the wall (x) is one leg of the right triangle formed with the 2-foot overhang as the hypotenuse. The measure of the apex angle (A) of this right triangle is determined by subtracting the measure of the base angle of the gable (E) from 90 degrees. See the illustration for clarification.

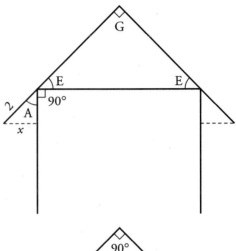

In the example, angle A equals 45 degrees. The right triangle is isosceles; therefore; the distance from the wall is equal to the distance along the wall. In this case, the Pythagorean theorem can be used to determine the distance the roof edge is from the wall.

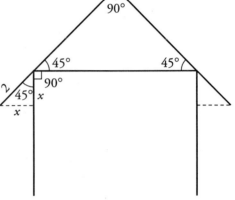

Since $a^2 + b^2 = c^2$,

then $x^2 + x^2 = 4$,

and $2x^2 = 4$,

or $x^2 = 2$.

Therefore, $x = {\sim}1.4$ feet.

The distance from the wall can also be determined using trigonometry. This technique can be applied in right triangle situations when only the apex angle and the hypotenuse are known. It is not expected that middle school students will use this technique.

$$\text{Sin } A = \frac{\text{leg opposite angle } A}{\text{hypotenuse}}$$

$$\text{Sin } 45° = \frac{\text{leg opposite angle } A}{\text{hypotenuse}}$$

$$0.707 = \frac{\text{leg opposite angle } A}{2}$$

$$1.414 = \text{leg opposite angle } A$$

Once each group has prepared a simple gable roof, students are asked to consider at least one other roof design before finalizing their presentation model. Student Sheet 5.3 provides examples and directions for alternate roof plans.

For some cabins, a modified gable roof with a non-centered ridge may be more suitable. For example, placing the ridge above the midpoint of the front extension on the cabin shown on Transparency Master 5.4 balances the effect and provides adequate pitch on each roof section. Maintaining the 9-foot vertical rise from the original gable roof gives about a 1:1 pitch on the steep side and a 1:3 on the other. Though they provide different effects, both roofs are considered by architects to be aesthetically pleasing.

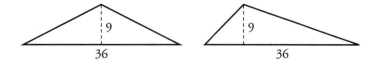

The triangle gables in both centered and non-centered ridge designs have different perimeters, but since they have the same base and height, their areas are equal. The side lengths of these triangles plus 2 feet represent the width of the 40-foot roof panels. The perimeter of the isosceles triangle is less than that of the scalene triangle pictured. Therefore, it is more cost-effective since the area of the roof panels for the isosceles gable is less than any gable roof with the same height and a non-centered ridge.

Once students find an appropriate best-fit rectangle for their cabin design, they may prefer the look of the shed roof. A shed roof represents half of a gable roof. Therefore, when determining pitch, the span of the best-fit rectangle is equivalent to the run. The minimum pitch for a standing seam metal shed roof is 1:4. The roof panel rests on congruent right triangles (on opposite sides of the building) and a rectangular wall extension with the same height as the triangles. As in the gable roof, this should not exceed the height of the building, unless a sleeping loft is added. For cabins designed to be one-story, a shed roof is not recommended when the span of the cabin is more than 36 feet, since that would require a rise of more than 9 feet.

An intersecting roof design is possible when the floor plan can be surrounded by two or more rectangles of best-fit that connect at right angles. This creates a major and a minor roof section and works best on L, T, U, and X-shaped designs. An intersecting roof minimizes excess overhang. Refer to Student Sheet 5.3 for building instructions.

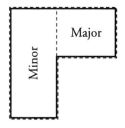

The main dimensions for an intersecting roof are estimated from the floor plan layout. It is general practice to have the same slope for all portions of a roof. When the roof sections have the same span and height, they meet at their ridges. If all roof sections have the same slope and one roof has a greater span than the other, they will not meet at the ridge. If the minor roof span is less than the major, it will intersect at a point on the roof below the major ridge. If the minor roof span is greater than the major, it will intersect at a point above the major ridge, leaving a triangular-shaped gap to enclose.

Students may also choose to adapt these plans to create their own roof design. Combining roof types, such as the shed and gable shown, may achieve a desired effect.

Use the Career Link "Carpenter to Contractor" at any time during the activity to enhance student interest.

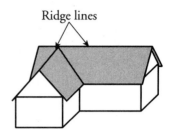

Ridge lines

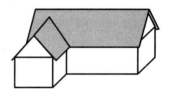

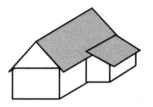

Presenting the Activity

Raising the Roof. Ask groups to discuss among themselves what purpose a roof serves. Then conduct a class discussion to elicit their responses. Once the discussion clearly determines the dual purpose of protecting and decorating a building, ask groups to describe or sketch the shapes and styles of roofs they may have seen in their neighborhoods, in the city, and finally in other parts of the world. During a summary discussion, sketch or list several of these on the board or overhead before asking which of the shapes seem appropriate for the camp setting and cabin designs.

Discuss whether a flat roof is appropriate for the cabin, and why it may not be. Find out if they have noticed buildings where the roof did not seem quite right for the situation, and ask why they thought so. Ask if it is possible for more than one roof style to suit a particular building. Have students give reasons for their responses.

Display Transparency Master 5.4 and ask groups to discuss how the different roof styles affect the aesthetics of the cabin model. Through this exchange, bring out their diverse opinions concerning how roof design alters appearance and influences appeal.

Distribute Student Sheet 5.1, grid paper, rulers, and protractors or Cuisenaire® angle rulers. Ask students to read and discuss the introduction in their groups, then highlight procedures and expectations during a class discussion. As they begin working, facilitate group interactions and, if necessary, assist them in assessing the best-fit rectangle for their floor plan. Ask how they will use additional living space that may be created by the excess overhang of the roof. Remind them to include this in their report from Student Sheet 4.2. Mention the possible need for support pillars, depending on the size of the overhang.

When all groups have had a chance to analyze and respond to questions 2 and 3, conduct a class discussion wherein participants clarify the terminology and procedures for determining the vertical rise for a particular pitch.

After students resume work on Student Sheet 5.1 to investigate aspects of pitch, ensure conclusions are based on analyzing appropriate and sufficient data. Some may want to draw gables with a 1:5 or 1:6 pitch for further comparison. Expect sound reasoning on each question and make suggestions for further explorations where necessary.

Conduct a summary discussion to bring out the relationships between span, pitch, vertical rise, ridge angle, cost, and effectiveness. Have various groups present and substantiate their findings, allowing others to question them or offer supportive data. Remarks may include that the ridge angle for any given pitch is constant regardless of the span; whereas the vertical rise for any given pitch varies according to the span. In this way, a steep pitch on a wide building is overwhelming in height, yet on a narrow building the height is in proportion. Lowering pitch lowers vertical rise and cost, but too low a pitch is also unappealing and inappropriate for snow.

After assessing which pitches they feel are acceptable for snow, explain that the building code for a standing seam metal roof allows a minimum 1:4 pitch. Ask what constitutes an appropriate vertical rise. When is it too high, or too low? Their concluding comments may agree with the professional recommendation that a vertical rise be less than the wall height for a one-story building.

Top It Off. Verify that each group has agreed on a reasonable pitch for the gable roof of their particular cabin before handing out Student Sheet 5.2, cardstock, scissors, and tape. Though the roof panels can be an alternate color, advise them to consider using the same color cardstock for the gables and walls. Support group efforts as they complete their gable roofs. Discuss the need to include triangular trusses for support. Be sure they understand that a truss is used as a brace for structural stability. Ask students to describe the various types of trusses they have seen.

Propose cutting one cardstock gable as a template for the remaining gable and trusses to increase accuracy, save time, and conserve paper (by joining gable and truss triangles on the cardboard to form parallelograms before cutting.) As they assess their completed roof, ask students if any support pillars seem necessary, or why they may not be needed. Talk about the number of trusses they used to support the roof. Tell them an architect would know the building codes and include the proper number.

Remind them that they will build at least one other roof type for their model before making a final selection for the presentation. Explain that directions are given for roof types displayed on Transparency Master 5.4, but they may choose to design their own.

Have copies of Student Sheet 5.3 available when students are ready to construct the second roof. Suggest that they build and try different roofs to analyze their appeal before attaching their final selection. It is possible that some groups will want to display more than one roof on their model during the presentation. Emphasize that the model is an important tool, allowing the client to visualize the building in its final state. Their ongoing reports from Student Sheet 4.2 should indicate how, and on what basis, they made their roof decisions.

Discussion Questions

1. What influence does climate have on roof design?

2. What influence does culture have on roof design?

3. How does pitch influence the purpose, appeal, and cost of a roof?

4. What effect does availability of materials have on roof design?

5. Measure the distance from the bottom edge of your roof to the wall.

   a. Is it the same on all sides? Why or why not?

   b. Is the length of the overhang equal to the distance from the wall?

   c. How does the pitch affect the distance the roof edge is from the wall?

Assessment Questions

1. Pitch, span, and rise!

   a. What happens to the vertical rise when various pitches are applied to a fixed roof span? Illustrate and explain your reasoning.

   b. What happens to the vertical rise when a fixed pitch is applied to various roof spans? Illustrate and explain your reasoning.

   c. How do you determine the pitch of a roof if you want a specific vertical rise on a variety of building spans? Illustrate and explain your reasoning.

2. What pitches could your cabin roof have in order for the vertical rise to be less than 10 feet? Explain your reasoning.

3. If a gable roof and a shed roof have the same span and height, how do the areas of the end triangles compare? Illustrate and explain your reasoning.

4. This is a final floor plan proposed for a camp cabin. In the drawing, $\frac{1}{4}$ inch = 2 feet. Design an appropriate roof for this cabin. Include the following:

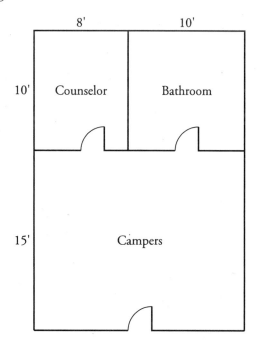

   a. The roof style you selected, and why.

   b The pitch you recommend, and why.

   c. A scale drawing of the gable design with its dimensions labeled.

   d. A scale drawing of the roof panel(s) with a 2-foot overhang represented on each side of the cabin. Label the dimensions.

Carpenter to Contractor

David Crocker is a building contractor who operates his own company, Odyssey Builders in Seattle, Washington. He specializes in building and remodeling homes of all sizes. Projects may range from a $20,000 foundation or structural upgrade for one client to a $600,000 remodel, where he is following an architect's plan for a complete remodel of a home.

David earned his undergraduate degree in geology in 1972. Because of his combined interests in applied mathematics and working with his hands, David took time from graduate school to work as a carpenter. He found he loved solving design and construction problems, and his reputation as a reliable and talented carpenter grew. Instead of returning to graduate school, David decided to acquire his contractor's license.

One day, an architect friend asked David to be the contractor on a major remodel he had designed. Though David was busy at the time on another project, his friend suggested he hire a separate crew and supervise them doing the actual work. David had been busy and content working on his own, and the idea of expanding his business hadn't occurred to him. After giving it some thought, he decided to do it. That's when he became an official contractor.

A contractor is responsible for executing an architect's vision. David especially enjoys it when the architect is doing something in a new way. This forces David to step outside of what he normally does and look at the project from a new perspective.

Another aspect of his job that David particularly likes is consulting with interior designers. An interior designer may have great design ideas for a space, but not necessarily know how to make it happen. In such a case, David hires an architect to analyze the space structurally and prepare plans based on the interior designer's sketch.

David usually coordinates four construction projects at a time. At each job site, he manages a crew of several carpenters. Working as a supervisor entails a lot of paperwork and continual assessment of the work at each site. David must also schedule meetings with clients, architects, building inspectors, and prospective customers. He must hire subcontractors who specialize in such things as plumbing, wiring, plastering, or painting and integrate them into project timelines. Ultimately, David is responsible for the completion and quality of employee's and subcontractor's work. He also deals with the client and architect on issues that arise during construction where design changes are considered that may require additional time and money.

Fortunately, technology is helping David. He would be lost without his computer to keep the information about each project current and organized. With the computer, he outlines the materials needed at each site and their costs, prepares a budget and a bid for the client, and prints project timelines. David also uses beepers and cell phones to stay in close contact with the lead carpenter at each site and to reach the architect or clients for quick consultations.

These days, when David looks at a home constructed by Odyssey Builders, he can no longer say he built it with his own hands, but he can say that he saw to it that the home was built well.

Pitch and Span

As a group, you will complete at least two different roof designs with a 2-foot overhang for your model and choose the type that best suits your cabin. After building a gable roof, your group may select another roof style to construct from the guidelines provided or create your own design.

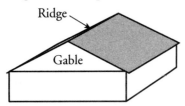

A gable roof consists of two sloping rectangles called *roof panels* that meet at the ridge. The triangles formed at opposite ends of the cabin are called *gables*.

1. Outline a best-fit rectangle that encloses your cabin floor plan. The best-fit rectangle forms the base of the roof.
   a. Is there more than one possible best-fit rectangle? Explain.

   b. How did your group determine the best-fit rectangle?

2. Gables are usually constructed on the shortest sides of the best-fit rectangle. The width of this side of the cabin is called the *span* of the cabin.
   a. Determine the span of your model.

   b. Half the span is called the *run*. What is the run of your model?

   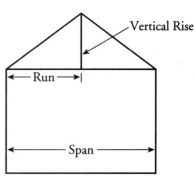

   c. Compute the actual span and run of your cabin.

   © Washington MESA Published by Dale Seymour Publications®

Pitch and Span

3. The height of the gable is called the *vertical rise*. The *pitch* of a roof refers to its slope and is expressed as the ratio *vertical rise:run*.
   a. What is the vertical rise for a gable with a 1:1 pitch on your cabin? Explain your reasoning.

   b. What is the vertical rise for a gable with a 1:2 pitch on your cabin? Explain your reasoning.

4. Each member of your group is to choose a different pitch from the list below and draw a prospective gable to scale on grid paper for the roof of your model. Let $\frac{1}{4}$ inch = 1 foot.
   a. 1:1 pitch   b. 1:2 pitch   c. 1:3 pitch   d. 1:4 pitch

5. Explain and illustrate how the pitch of a gable affects its vertical rise.

6. Explain how the pitch of a gable affects the cost of the roof.

7. Cut out and carefully hold each of the four gables on the appropriate edge of the cabin model for comparison.
   a. Do any appear too tall? Explain.

   b. Do any appear too short? Explain.

   c. Do any appear just right? Explain.

Pitch and Span

8. The ridge angle is formed where the two roof panels meet. Measure the ridge angle for each pitch, using the gables you drew, and record these measures in the table below. Explain how changing the pitch affects the ridge angle.

Pitch	Span	Ridge Angle
1:1		
1:2		
1:3		
1:4		

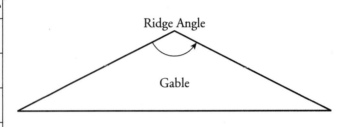

9. Gather data from another group whose model has a different span, and record their ridge angles for the same pitches. If the span changes, what happens to the ridge angle for a pitch of 1:1, 1:2, 1:3, and 1:4? Explain your reasoning.

Pitch	Span	Ridge Angle
1:1		
1:2		
1:3		
1:4		

Pitch and Span

10. Use your work with gables to answer these questions:
    a. Which slopes seem best for snow? Explain your reasoning.

    b. Which slopes are not good for snow? Explain your reasoning.

11. Within your group, decide which pitch to use for your gable roof. Explain your selection.

Top It Off

Follow these steps to construct a gable roof for your cabin model.

Gables

1. Once you have decided on the pitch for your gable roof, use the corresponding grid pattern to draw and cut two identical triangular gables out of cardstock.

2. Use a gable as a template, and cut out 1 or 2 cardstock trusses to use for support along the inside of the roof.

Roof Panels

3. The client has decided on a 2-foot overhang for the cabin roof. Represent this on your floor plan by drawing a $\frac{1}{2}$-inch border around the rectangle of best fit. This border rectangle closely approximates the roof base.

4. Measure the length of the non-gable side of the roof base on your floor plan to determine the length of each panel.

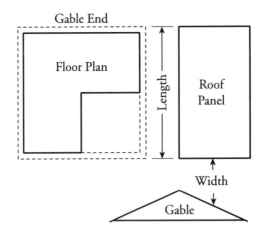

5. To determine the width of each panel, measure the side length of the triangular gable and add $\frac{1}{2}$ inch to allow for the overhang.

© Washington MESA Published by Dale Seymour Publications®

Top It Off

6. Use these dimensions to cut two identical roof panels out of cardstock. Hinge them together with tape on one side to form the ridge.

Assembling the Roof

7. Draw lines $\frac{1}{2}$ inch inside the gable ends of the panels as guidelines for securing the gables to the panels.

8. Draw appropriate guidelines on the panels for attaching the trusses.

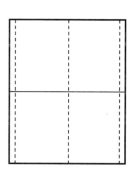

9. Align the peak of each gable and truss with the ridge and use the guidelines to tape one side of each gable in place on the roof panel.

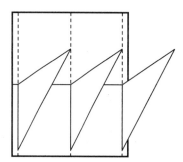

10. Fold up the roof and tape the remaining side of the gables and trusses to the hinged roof panel to form the ridge angles, and complete the gable roof.

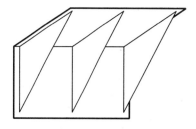

11. Place the completed roof on top of your model without attaching it.

Styles and Selections

Note: Study all three additional roof options described here, and then select one that seems appropriate for your cabin. Build it, then compare and contrast it with your gable roof.

Non-Centered Ridge Roof

In a non-centered ridge roof, the gables are not isosceles triangles, and each panel has a different pitch.

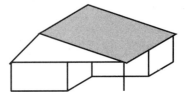

Gables

1. On grid paper, draw the base of the gable equal to the span of your model.

2. Decide where along the span you want to locate the highest point of the roof. Using the same height as your original gable roof, draw in the vertical rise perpendicular to the base of the triangle at this point.

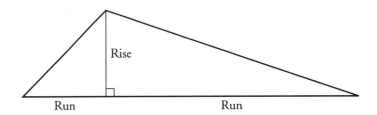

3. Complete the triangle and determine the pitch of each panel. Decide if each pitch is adequate. If not, revise the gable by changing the location of the highest point or by changing the height itself.

Roof Construction

4. Once you have determined an appropriate non-centered ridge, follow steps 1 through 11 on Student Sheet 5.2 to complete the roof. When constructing the roof panels, each rectangle will have the same length, but different widths. Their widths are determined by the side lengths of the gable.

Styles and Selections

Shed Roof

A shed roof is sloped, but it does not have a ridge. It resembles one side of a gable roof.

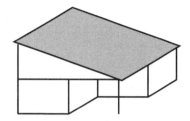

Shed Ends

1. Design the right triangle for the shed ends by drawing its base on grid paper equal to the span of your model.

2. For a shed roof, the span of the cabin is also the run, which is used for determining pitch. Decide the vertical rise that will provide an adequate pitch with the given span and still be aesthetically pleasing.

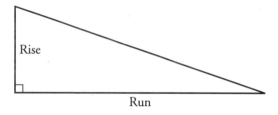

3. Construct the height to form a right triangle with the base.

4. Use this as a pattern to cut right triangles out of cardstock for the two shed ends and one or two support trusses.

Wall Extension

5. Design the rectangular wall extension on grid paper, and cut it out of cardstock. Its width is equal to the vertical rise of the roof, and its length is the side measure between the shed ends on the best-fit rectangle surrounding your floor plan.

6. Tape the three roof structure pieces together.

Styles and Selections

Shed Roof (cont'd)

Roof Panel

7. The total length of your roof panel is equal to the length of the wall extension plus 1 inch for the overhang ($\frac{1}{2}$ inch on each side).

8. To determine the width, measure the length of the longest side of the right triangle and add 1 inch to it for the overhang.

9. Design the roof panel on grid paper, and cut it out of cardstock.

Assembling the Roof

10. Draw a line $\frac{1}{2}$ inch inside the edge along three sides of the panel as a guideline for securing the roof structure.

11. Attach the roof panel to the wall extension.

12. Fold up the roof structure and tape the shed ends in place.

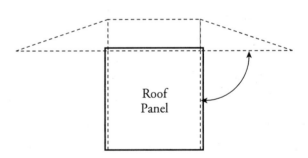

13. Add trusses.

14. Place the completed roof on top of your model without attaching it.

Styles and Selections

Intersecting Roof

An intersecting roof has at least two sections. The
major section is a gable roof. Where the minor roof
intersects it, the ridge lines are perpendicular and
aligned if their heights are equal.

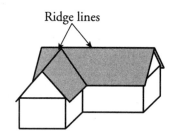

Ridge lines

Floor Plan

1. Redraw the perimeter of your cabin floor plan onto grid paper.

2. Outline at least two rectangles of best-fit that meet at right angles
   on your floor plan.

3. Surround the perimeter of the best-fit rectangles with a $\frac{1}{2}$-inch
   border approximating the 2-foot overhang and the roof line.

Major Roof

4. Construct a gable roof with an adequate pitch over the major section.

5. Place the roof on the model and make two $\frac{1}{2}$-inch slits
   in the appropriate locations on the roof panel to allow
   it to slip into place on the cabin model.

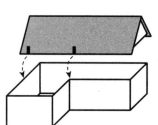

Minor Roof

6. Construct a gable for the minor span with the same
   pitch as the major roof.

7. The panels on the minor roof
   are right trapezoids. Their width
   is equal to the side length of
   the minor gable plus $\frac{1}{2}$ inch
   for the overhang.

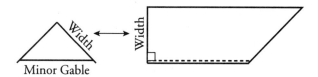

Width

Width

Minor Gable

Styles and Selections

8. On the floor plan diagram, draw in the roof ridges and indicate their point of intersection.

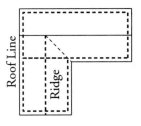

9. Measure the lengths of the minor ridge and the minor roof line on your floor plan as illustrated. These represent the parallel sides on the trapezoid panel.

10. On grid paper, construct the three known sides of the right trapezoid and connect the endpoints to complete the panel design.

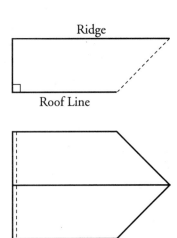

11. Cut two identical trapezoid roof panels out of cardstock, and hinge them with tape at the ridge.

12. Draw a $\frac{1}{2}$-inch line from the gable end on the panels as a guideline for securing the gable. Attach the minor gable to the roof panels.

13. Place the minor roof on the model and secure it to the gable roof to complete the intersecting roof.

Raise the Roof

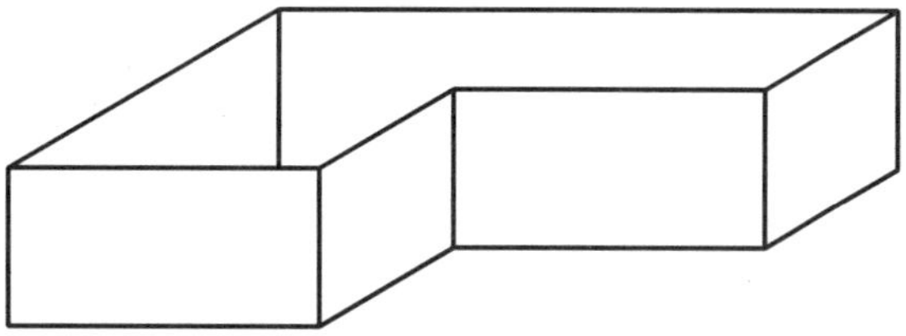

Cabin Model

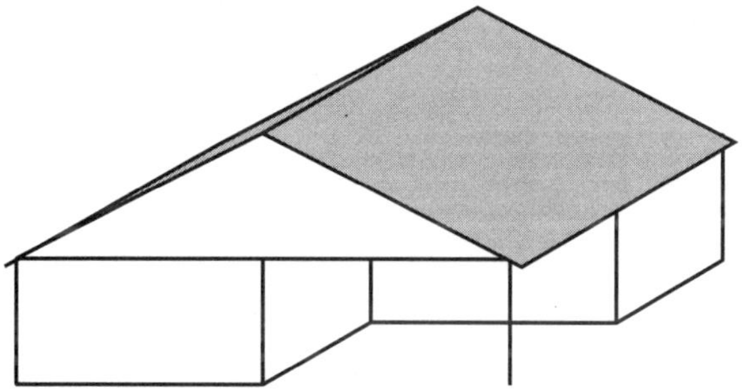

Gable Roof

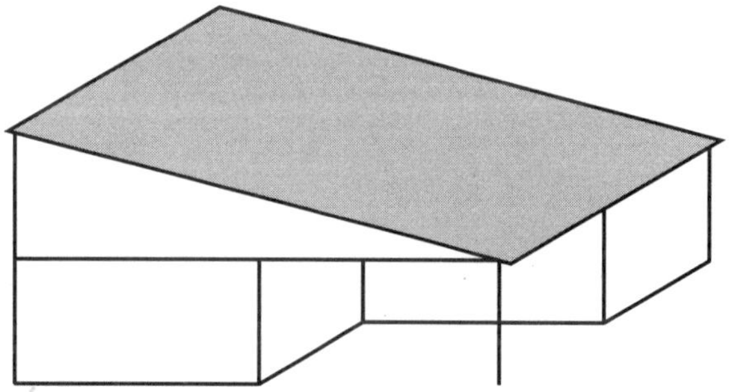

Shed Roof

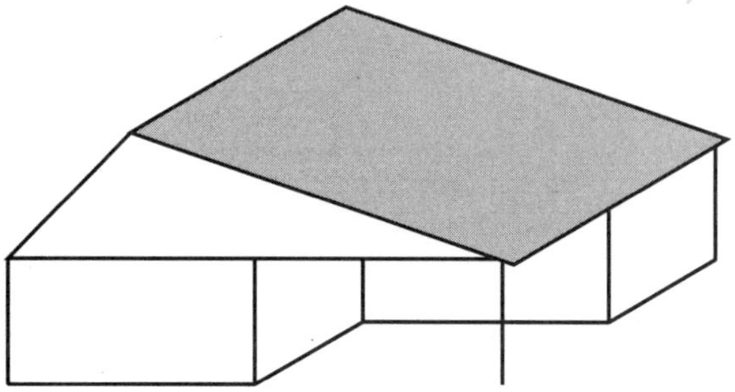

Gable Roof
with Non-Centered Ridge

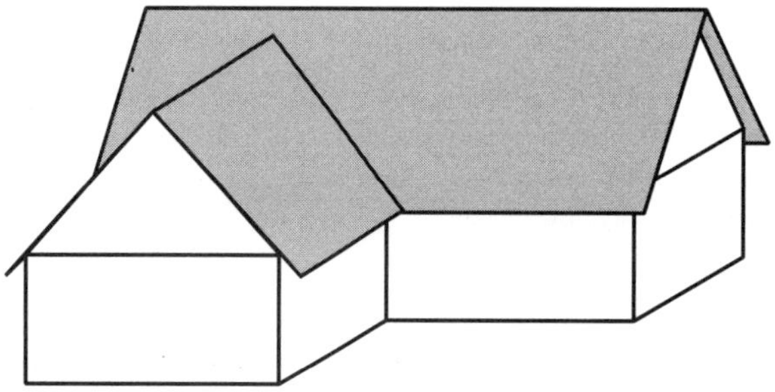

Intersecting Roof

FAMILY
ACTIVITY

PROJECT
PLAYHOUSE

Overview

Students are introduced to CASA (Court Appointed Special Advocates), an organization that provides volunteers who represent the interests and needs of abused and neglected children in court. CASA programs throughout the country auction or raffle off playhouses as an annual fund-raising event. In this activity, each family brainstorms ideas to design a children's playhouse and builds a scale model of it with the intent of donating the design to CASA or a local organization of their choosing that will auction the completed playhouse to benefit their programs.

Time. Approximately six hours, following Activity 5.

Purpose. Students apply architectural procedures as they create and design a playhouse with their families. By donating their project, students recognize how they are able to support the community in which they live.

Materials. *For each student:*

◆ Interest Link, CASA: An Advocate for Children

◆ Family Activity Sheets 1–2

For each family:

◆ $\frac{1}{4}$-inch grid paper

◆ Paper for drawings

◆ Cardstock for the model

◆ Scissors

◆ Tape

◆ Ruler

◆ Calculator

◆ X-Acto® knife

◆ 12-inch by 12-inch cardboard base

For the teacher:

◆ Transparencies of Family Activity Sheets 1–2

Getting Ready

1. Review the materials list and decide which items you can supply to families, if necessary.

2. Duplicate the Interest Link and Family Activity Sheets 1–2.

3. Prepare a transparency of Family Activity Sheets 1–2.

Background Information

The notion of selling children's playhouses to benefit a charity has been used by several organizations over the years. One of these is CASA, Court Appointed Special Advocates. A CASA volunteer upholds the best interests of abused and neglected children in court. (See Interest Link). From 1991 to 1995, an estimated thirty CASA programs throughout the country conducted successful playhouse fund-raisers. A project like this can capture an individual's imagination and therefore inspire involvement and action in the community.

This activity involves the family in designing and building a model of a proposed playhouse, then discussing how best to use the plans to benefit a school or community organization. Here are a few suggestions students and their families might consider.

- Select one or more of the class plans to build with parent/school involvement and raffle it off to benefit the school.

- Prepare a booklet of the class plans and send them to a local CASA program or other organization to build and use as a fund-raising event.

- Involve the whole school in selecting one or more class models to build as a school community and donate the playhouse to a local day care or neighborhood park.

- All of the above!

The suggested time for this activity is six hours; the time required will vary from family to family. Give students a reasonable time period, perhaps a week spanning a weekend, to complete the assignment. They will need this to arrange adequate family time to work on the project.

Presenting the Activity

Ask students if they know why the Girl Scouts sell cookies. Besides money, some may suggest recognition and advertising of their organization, as well as a community reminder of who they are. Have them suggest how the organization uses the profits and what might happen if they did not have the cookie money. Inquire as to the type of fund-raising techniques used by other organizations with which they are familiar, and what purposes they serve. Allow the discussion to generate several ideas before distributing the Interest Link "CASA: An Advocate for Children."

Have students read the Interest Link and discuss it in their groups, before initiating a class discussion to clarify the project and respond to questions. Let them know they will be designing a playhouse with their families, building a model of it, and deciding what to do with the playhouse plans as a class. Use the background suggestions and initiate a discussion to solicit student ideas about where to donate their plans—to a potential fund-raising event for a local organization or to their school. Ask them to ponder the various possibilities, to discuss them with their families, and to consider the options carefully as they are working on the project.

Distribute Family Activity Sheets 1–2 and have students read and discuss them in their groups. Provide time for discussion and clarification of your expectations. If students want to use cardstock for their models, decide how much of your supply to allot each family. Explain that on the day the project is due, they will display their playhouse models in class, and each student will give a presentation to describe their experience.

Resume small-group discussions on what to do with the playhouse plans throughout the project time period as appropriate or after their completion to narrow down the choices and make decisions. As a class, determine how to carry out the plan or plans.

Discussion Questions

1. Did you use perimeter and area relationships in your design process? If so, where? If not, why not?

2. Did you modify or revise your original playhouse ideas during the design process? If so, describe the changes and why you made them.

3. Decide with your group whether the models presented satisfy the following criteria:

   a. Playhouse will be a safe place to go for privacy and for friends to gather.

   b. Playhouse will be cost effective.

   c. Playhouse will be aesthetically pleasing.

CASA: An Advocate for Children

In Spanish, *casa* means house or home. CASA is an organization that derives its name from an acronym for its members, Court Appointed Special Advocates, trained community volunteers who uphold the best interests of abused and neglected children in court.

In 1978, Seattle Judge David Soukup was increasingly troubled. Was he making the right decisions for the abused and neglected children who came before him? He often could not be sure. There was not enough background information. Attorneys and social workers were usually too busy to provide it.

Late one anguished, wakeful night, Judge Soukup conceived the idea of a new kind of advocate for children. Concerned citizen volunteers could be trained to help review the cases of individual children, and return to him with recommendations. A CASA volunteer would represent the child's interests until a safe, nurturing, permanent home could be found. The idea was embraced in Seattle, and spread with stunning speed around the country.

Today, just a decade and a half later, there are 40,000 CASA volunteers in 50 states, working in over 680 CASA programs. Some 150,000 children each year have the benefit of **CASA** advocacy. Maintaining and building this program requires financial resources as well as volunteers. Many of the CASA programs have begun building *casas for CASA*—imaginative playhouses put together with talent, time, and materials donated by the community and then raffled or auctioned to benefit the CASA programs.

Nathan Pinney

The employees at Keystone Home Builders in Keystone, Kentucky, wanted to plan and build a playhouse for their local Boone County CASA auction, but were having trouble visualizing an idea. Then it hit them—who better to design a children's playhouse than a child. Eleven-year-old Nathan Pinney, whose father is part-owner of the company, designed a tugboat playhouse for the company to build. His design includes a sandbox play area on one side of the tug. The green

PROJECT PLAYHOUSE **123**

Student Playhouse Model

and white boat features rope railings and an antique steering wheel donated to the project. It has an authentic boat bell and a cushioned bench with a table inside. It is constructed of pressure-treated lumber and redwood donated by a local lumber and supply company.

In Seattle, architecture students at the University of Washington created fifty original playhouse designs and assembled the plans for them into a booklet. Carpenters and volunteers across the country will build the playhouses from donated materials based on the instructions in the design booklet. The finished products will be raffled off to benefit the more than 640 CASA chapters.

One good way to find out about CASA groups in your area is to check the World Wide Web site http://www.nationalcasa.org.

Playhouse Plans

A playhouse is a safe place to go for privacy and for friends to hang out. As a family, you will design a children's playhouse and build a scale model of it. Read through the activity sheets before beginning in order to understand the procedures and expectations.

Design Criteria

- The playhouse has to fit onto an 8-foot by 8-foot site.
- The overall height, including the roof, cannot exceed 8 feet.
- Remember, this is for children, and it needs to be safe for the age child who will use it.
- Windows may be left as open areas or made of acrylic. Wooden shutters are an option.
- No plumbing or electricity.

1. Read and discuss the Interest Link, CASA: An Advocate for Children.

2. Use your imaginations and brainstorm several ideas for a children's playhouse. Follow these steps:
   a. Clearly state the purpose for the playhouse you will design.
   b. Give everyone a chance to suggest ideas.
   c. Have someone record the ideas on paper.
   d. Do not judge or eliminate any ideas during this session.

3. Look closely at the ideas proposed, and pick one your family thinks will work best. Ask:
   a. Does the idea fit the playhouse purpose?
   b. Will it meet the design criteria?
   c. How will it appeal to children?
   d. How will it appeal to adults?
   e. How does it appeal to each family member?
   f. Is it a safe place for children?

Playhouse Plans

4. If you are able to give satisfactory responses to the questions in number 3, you probably have a creative and workable playhouse proposal. If not, select a different idea from your brainstorming session and repeat question 3.

5. Once you make a design decision, prepare detailed playhouse plans in the form of sketches, scale drawings on grid paper or floor plans with dimensions, and a roof plan. Include doorway and window locations, as well as ideas for interior furnishings.

Playhouse Product

Materials you may need include:
- Ruler
- Cardstock for the model
- Scissors
- Tape
- Calculator
- X-Acto® knife
- 12-inch by 12-inch cardboard base on which to mount the model

1. Let 1 inch = 1 foot. Construct a scale model of your proposed playhouse, using cardstock or other appropriate materials.
   a. Cut out a base for each level of the playhouse that duplicates the final floor plan.
   b. Cut out the walls and indicate the location of windows and doorways.
   c. Tape the wall pieces together side-by-side to form a continuous strip.
   d. Position the walls on the base, but without attaching them.
   e. Decide if you want to make any window, doorway, or height adjustments.
   f. Cut out windows and doorways before attaching the wall strip to the base.

2. Examine the roof possibilities for your playhouse. Unlike the camp cabin roofs, the roof on a playhouse often becomes an extension of the play area.
   a. Decide if your roof design is safe.
   b. Determine if your roof area requires railings as well as a stairway or ladder for access from below.
   c. Construct the roof. Secure it in place so that it can be opened for viewing the playhouse interior, if desired.

3. Using the scale 1 inch = 1 foot, outline the 8-foot by 8-foot site onto the cardboard base. Mount your model onto this base within the site boundaries.

Playhouse Product

4. Discuss how to use your playhouse plans. This could include donating them to a specific organization or school for a fund-raising project.

5. Prepare a presentation report for the class that includes how you decided on the final design, along with the completed playhouse model, and the plans used to build it.

COMPLETED
STUDENT
SHEETS

Camp Cabins

A client planning to build a year-round environmental camp for middle school students is asking your architectural firm to submit design plans for a one story cabin that sleeps ten campers. It should include a bathroom with two toilets, four sinks and two showers, as well as a separate private sleeping area for the cabin counselor. Your client wants to provide campers with a pleasant yet simple and rustic structure that emphasizes the outdoor experience.

The 164-acre, gently sloping wooded site has two streams draining into a small lake for nonmotorized recreation. The weather in fall and spring can be cool and damp, while summers are moderately hot. Light snowfall and wind are common in winter with temperatures generally above 20 degrees Fahrenheit.

As with all clients, keeping finances reasonable is a concern. Once they choose a design, they plan to build fifteen identical cabins so that 150 students can attend each session. They want a cabin that suits their needs, is aesthetically pleasing, and gives them the most for their money.

1. An architect must consider the basic needs that a design will fulfill. With your group, determine the number of rooms to include in the cabin design and explain the purpose of each one.
Responses will vary, but should include saying that the cabin design includes a minimum of three rooms—one large room for sleeping ten campers, a bathroom for eleven people, and a separate room for the counselor.

2. Architects use flow diagrams to show the general location of each room in a very rough form. These drawings use circular shapes to illustrate design ideas. One possibility is shown for a three-room cabin. Sketch a variety of flow diagrams to record possible cabin room arrangements for your client.
Responses will vary, but might include some of the following:

Dwelling Designs

A *floor plan* is a scale drawing. It is the view you would see if you cut the roof off of a building and looked down on the rooms from above. A floor plan shows the layout of each room; and often how it is furnished. Including the furniture gives a better indication of the size of the room. A floor plan is used in estimating costs and in the actual construction of a building.

1. With your group, sketch onto a transparency possible floor plans that this flow diagram could represent.

   a. How many different designs based on this flow diagram are possible? Explain.
   There are an infinite number of possible designs. This is because the shape and size of a room are not determined by the flow diagram. Flow diagrams only show the location of rooms and give a sense of relative size.

   b. How did you indicate doorways in your sketches?
   Responses will vary.

   c. How did you show window locations in your sketches?
   Responses will vary.

2. Divide into two teams. List the members of each team. Each team will select one of your preferred flow diagrams from question 3 on Student Sheet 1.1 and create a cabin floor plan, following the instructions below. The group will preview both plans.
   Responses will vary.

3. Use grid paper to draw the floor plan for your proposed cabin. Let $\frac{1}{4}$ inch = 1 foot. Be sure to indicate the cabin dimensions along the perimeter and draw to scale the location of doorways, windows, furniture, and bathroom facilities.

Money Matters

3. Are the expense differences significant? Explain your reasoning.
Responses will vary.

4. Will buildings with the same square footage always cost the same? Explain.
Not necessarily. If one cabin has a smaller perimeter than the other, it will cost less to build.

5. According to the table, does a larger cabin always cost more than a smaller cabin? Provide examples to support your reasoning.
Not necessarily. A smaller cabin with extensive perimeter could cost more to build than a larger cabin.

6. What are possible causes for the variation in cabin expenses?
Responses may include changes in either area or perimeter.

7. How many of the proposed cabin designs will cost the client more than your design? Less than your design?
Responses will vary.

8. Make a scatter plot of the class cabin data that relates the cost of each cabin to the square feet it provides. With your group, discuss what it shows, and then record your observations.
Responses will vary, but the scatter plot may show that there are some cabins with the same cost that have different areas, and there are cabins with the same area that have different costs.

9. Are there any design changes you could make to increase the chance of your cabin being selected?
Responses will vary.

10. Besides cost, what else might influence the client's choice?
Responses will vary. Answers may include the fact that the client may also be influenced by aesthetics, that is, whether the design is appealing, and also by whether the design seems to function well for the intended purpose.

Expense Estimates

5. Is it fair to compare overall costs to determine which cabin is the better buy? Explain your reasoning.
Responses will vary.

6. Another way to compare cabin costs is to analyze the expenses per square foot.
   a. Calculate the cost per square foot of floor space for your cabin design, and explain your procedures.
   Responses will vary.
   b. How does the cost per square foot for your design compare to the cost per square foot of the other design in your group?
   Responses will vary.
   c. Do the total cost and the cost per square foot give the same comparison? Explain your reasoning.
   No. It is possible for a cabin that has a greater total cost to cost less per square foot to build than a cabin that has a lesser total cost.

Form Follows Function

1. Use 40 square tiles to represent 40 acres. Work with a partner to design a shape that gives the greatest perimeter possible when joining squares edge-to-edge.
   a. Record the result on grid paper, and use a colored pen to highlight the perimeter.
      Responses will vary.
   b. Explain how you know that your design has the greatest perimeter possible.
      To have the greatest perimeter possible, each tile, except for the two end tiles, has only two edges connected to other tiles and the two end tiles have only one edge connected to another tile.
   c. Is this a good design for the animal preserve? Why or why not?
      Not necessarily. Depending on the types of animals, it may not provide adequate places for privacy away from human view or a large enough open space for animals to gather in groups.
   d. Determine the perimeter of your design in unit lengths.
      The perimeter will be 82 units in length.
   e. If a design has the greatest perimeter possible, is it unique? Explain your reasoning.
      No. There are many possible variations with each one adhering to the specifications from question 1b above.

2. Together with your partner, design a shape that has the least perimeter possible.
   a. Record the result on grid paper, and use a colored pen to highlight the perimeter.
      Responses will vary. The least possible perimeter is 26 units.
   b. Explain how you know that your design has the least perimeter possible.
      A polyomino preserve has the least possible perimeter when the maximum number of tiles are connected by as many edges as possible.

Species Survival Site

3. Each square tile represents 1 acre, or 43,560 square feet.
   a. How many feet does the length of one edge of a square tile represent? Explain your reasoning.
      The length that one edge on the square tile represents about 209 feet.
      Explanations will vary.
   b. In order to visualize this distance, find something that is about the same length that one edge of a square tile represents. Describe it.
      Responses will vary. A suggested point of reference is approximately the length of 3 school buses aligned end-to-end. (1 bus = 66 feet.)

4. How might the shape of the 164-acre environmental campsite affect your design decision?
   Responses will vary, but the preserve design must fit within the boundaries of the property.

5. Select one of your animal preserve designs to present, and list the features that make it preferable to the client.
   Responses will vary.

Polyomino Perimeters

Polyominos are shapes made by joining squares edge-to-edge. Work with your group to examine the possible perimeters for polyominos with a given area.

1. Use five square tiles, each with a side length of 1 unit.

   a. Rearrange the square tiles to find polyominos representing every possible perimeter. Record the shapes and their perimeters on grid paper.
   Responses will vary.

   b. What is the area of each polyomino you recorded?
   Each bas an area of 5 square units.

   c. Based on the data, what observations can you make about the perimeters?
   Responses may include a) there are 2 possible perimeters; b) the possible perimeters are 10 or 12 units; c) there are several designs possible when P = 12, but there is only one when P = 10.

2. Repeat the above process using one, then two, then three, and finally four square tiles.
   See Polyomino Perimeters Solution table (page 134) for data.

3. Prepare a table with three columns to organize the data recorded on grid paper. Label the columns *Number of Tiles*, *Area* (square units), and *Possible Perimeters* (units). For each number of tiles, list the perimeters in order from least to greatest.
   See Polyomino Perimeters Solution table (page 134) for data.

4. Based on these results, predict the possible perimeters for polyominos using 6 square tiles. Explain your reasoning.
   Responses will vary.

5. Repeat the process from question 1 to test your perimeter predictions for 6 square tiles. Then record your findings in the table you prepared.
   See Polyomino Perimeters Solution table (page 134) for data.

6. Predict possible perimeters for polyominos made with 7, 8, 9, and 10 square tiles. Then test your theories by repeating the process from question 1. Be sure to add this information to your table.
   Responses will vary.

Form Follows Function

c. Is this a good design for an animal preserve? Why or why not?
   Not necessarily. It may not provide adequate viewing areas or provide private spaces for animals to separate from each other.
   Responses will vary.

d. Determine the perimeter of your design in unit lengths.

e. If a design has the least perimeter possible, is it unique? Explain your reasoning.
   No. There are several variations possible, though not as many as preserves made with the maximum perimeter.

3. How does the perimeter of the animal preserve you designed compare to the design with the greatest perimeter and the design with the least perimeter?
   Responses will vary.

4. Does the shape of the animal preserve affect the cost of building it? Explain your reasoning.
   Possibly. As the perimeter increases, so does the cost of materials and construction time needed to build the added barriers.

5. What does the phrase *form follows function* suggest to you?
   Responses will vary, but might imply that the architect's design configuration corresponds to the structure's intended purpose.

COMPLETED STUDENT SHEETS   133

Polyomino Perimeters (student-generated table)

Polyomino Perimeters Solutions

Number of Tiles	Area (sq. units)	Possible Perimeters (units)
1	1	4
2	2	6
3	3	8
4	4	8, 10
5	5	10, 12
6	6	10, 12, 14
7	7	12, 14, 16
8	8	12, 14, 16, 18
9	9	12, 14, 16, 18, 20
10	10	14, 16, 18, 20, 22
11	11	14, 16, 18, 20, 22, 24
12	12	14, 16, 18, 20, 22, 24, 26
13	13	16, 18, 20, 22, 24, 26, 28
14	14	16, 18, 20, 22, 24, 26, 28, 30
15	15	16, 18, 20, 22, 24, 26, 28, 30, 32
16	16	16, 18, 20, 22, 24, 26, 28, 30, 32, 34
17	17	18, 20, 22, 24, 26, 28, 30, 32, 34, 36
18	18	18, 20, 22, 24, 26, 28, 30, 32, 34, 36, 38
19	19	18, 20, 22, 24, 26, 28, 30, 32, 34, 36, 38, 40
20	20	18, 20, 22, 24, 26, 28, 30, 32, 34, 36, 38, 40, 42
21	21	20, 22, 24, 26, 28, 30, 32, 34, 36, 38, 40, 42, 44
22	22	20, 22, 24, 26, 28, 30, 32, 34, 36, 38, 40, 42, 44, 46
23	23	20, 22, 24, 26, 28, 30, 32, 34, 36, 38, 40, 42, 44, 46, 48
24	24	20, 22, 24, 26, 28, 30, 32, 34, 36, 38, 40, 42, 44, 46, 48, 50
25	25	20, 22, 24, 26, 28, 30, 32, 34, 36, 38, 40, 42, 44, 46, 48, 50, 52
26	26	22, 24, 26, 28, 30, 32, 34, 36, 38, 40, 42, 44,46, 48, 50, 52, 54
27	27	22, 24, 26, 28, 30, 32, 34, 36, 38, 40, 42, 44,46, 48, 50, 52, 54, 56
28	28	22, 24, 26, 28, 30, 32, 34, 36, 38, 40, 42, 44,46, 48, 50, 52, 54, 56, 58
29	29	22, 24, 26, 28, 30, 32, 34, 36, 38, 40, 42, 44,46, 48, 50, 52, 54, 56, 58, 60

Polyomino Perimeters

7. At this point, what conclusions can you make about the possible perimeters for a polyomino?

    Responses will vary, but they may include a) the number of possible perimeters increases as the number of tiles increases; b) the maximum perimeter is twice the number of tiles plus two; c) the possible perimeters are always consecutive even numbers.

8. What patterns do you notice in the table?

    Responses will vary, but may include a) the number of tiles is equivalent to the area in square units; b) beginning with 1 tile, as the minimum perimeter increases, the number of possible areas repeats in a pattern of 1,1, 2, 2, 3, 3, 4, 4 . . . .

9. Make the following perimeter predictions for polyominos made with 26 tiles, and explain your reasoning.

    a. The longest possible perimeter.

    Responses will vary.

    b. The shortest possible perimeter.

    Responses will vary.

    c. Every possible perimeter.

    Responses will vary.

10. Continue to make predictions with your group as you investigate the minimum, maximum, and every possible perimeter for polyominos made with 11, 12, 13, 14, 15 . . . , 40 tiles. Be sure to verify your conclusions and record the data in the table.

    Responses will vary. See Polyomino Perimeters Solution table (page 134) for data.

11. Write a one-page report that summarizes your procedures, observations, and conclusions. Explain how an architect might use this information when developing an animal preserve.

    Responses will vary.

Plot Plan

3. Explain how you can rearrange squares on your 40-acre design without changing the perimeter.

   If a section is cut off from the preserve by disconnecting one or more edges and this same number of edges is reattached elsewhere on the preserve, the perimeters will be the same,

4. There are 5,280 feet in one mile.

   a. Do you think that the preserve perimeter is more than or less than one mile? Explain your reasoning.
   Responses will vary.

   b. Determine the actual perimeter of your animal preserve in miles. Show your process.
   Responses will vary.

   c. Estimate the time it will take to walk around your preserve. Explain your reasoning.
   Responses will vary.

5. Draw a $\frac{1}{2}$-mile path on the plot plan from the lake to the location of one cabin.

6. Mark the location of each of the remaining fourteen cabins on the plot plan with an X. Then write a short report explaining your recommendations to the client.

Polyomino Perimeters (Student-generated table)

Polyomino Perimeters Solutions

Number of Tiles	Area (sq. units)	Possible Perimeters (units)
30	30	22, 24, 26, 28, 30, 32, 34, 36, 38, 40, 42, 44,46, 48, 50, 52, 54, 56, 58, 60, 62
31	31	24, 26, 28, 30, 32, 34, 36, 38, 40, 42, 44,46, 48, 50, 52, 54, 56, 58, 60, 62, 64
32	32	24, 26, 28, 30, 32, 34, 36, 38, 40, 42, 44,46, 48, 50, 52, 54, 56, 58, 60, 62, 64, 66
33	33	24, 26, 28, 30, 32, 34, 36, 38, 40, 42, 44,46, 48, 50, 52, 54, 56, 58, 60, 62, 64, 66, 68
34	34	24, 26, 28, 30, 32, 34, 36, 38, 40, 42, 44,46, 48, 50, 52, 54, 56, 58, 60, 62, 64, 66, 68, 70
35	35	24, 26, 28, 30, 32, 34, 36, 38, 40, 42, 44,46, 48, 50, 52, 54, 56, 58, 60, 62, 64, 66, 68, 70, 72
36	36	24, 26, 28, 30, 32, 34, 36, 38, 40, 42, 44,46, 48, 50, 52, 54, 56, 58, 60, 62, 64, 66, 68, 70, 72, 74
37	37	26, 28, 30, 32, 34, 36, 38, 40, 42, 44,46, 48, 50, 52, 54, 56, 58, 60, 62, 64, 66, 68, 70, 72, 74, 76
38	38	26, 28, 30, 32, 34, 36, 38, 40, 42, 44,46, 48, 50, 52, 54, 56, 58, 60, 62, 64, 66, 68, 70, 72, 74, 76, 78
39	39	26, 28, 30, 32, 34, 36, 38, 40, 42, 44,46, 48, 50, 52, 54, 56, 58, 60, 62, 64, 66, 68, 70, 72, 74, 76, 78, 80
40	40	26, 28, 30, 32, 34, 36, 38, 40, 42, 44,46, 48, 50, 52, 54, 56, 58, 60, 62, 64, 66, 68, 70, 72, 74, 76, 78, 80, 82

Cottage Choices

2. Let the length of one tile equal 6 feet.
   a. Determine the number of square feet that a tile represents, and explain your reasoning.
   Each tile represents 36 square feet. The area of each tile can be found by multiplying length times width.

   b. Use this scale to calculate and record the actual square footage for each cottage floor plan drawn in question 1a.

Number of Tiles	6	7	8	9	10	11	12
Square Feet	216	252	288	324	360	396	432

3. The interior wall expense has a minor influence on construction costs, and it is often excluded from initial estimates. Without considering interior wall expenses, use the price estimates below to calculate costs for each cottage area. Use your data to complete the table on the next page and calculate the cost per square foot for each area. Round costs to the nearest dollar.

Expense Estimates

Floors	$9.75 per square foot
10-Foot-High Exterior Walls	$140.00 per linear foot
Roof	1.5 times the floor cost

COMPLETED STUDENT SHEET 3.1

Cottage Choices

The master plan for the camp includes small guest cottages to be used by visiting zoo personnel or environmental instructors. Each cabin will accommodate one or two people. Because perimeter influences cost, the client has asked that the architects investigate various floor plans for a guest cottage that has a specific perimeter.

1. Use square tiles along with the table you prepared for Student Sheet 2.3 to design polyomino cottages that have a perimeter of 14 units and different areas.

   a. Draw a floor plan on grid paper to represent every possible polyomino area with a perimeter equivalent to 14 units. List the possible areas.
   Actual polyomino shapes will vary, but they should represent areas of 6, 7, 8, 9, 10, 11, and 12 square units.

   b. Is there more than one design for each possible area representation with this perimeter? Explain.
   Yes, except for the 3-by-4 rectangle with an area of 12 square units.

   c. Which floor plan do you prefer? Explain the reasons for your preference.
   Responses will vary.

   d. Based on your designs, predict which cottage is the least expensive to build and explain your reasoning.
   Responses will vary, but may suggest when A = 6 square units. Since all of the designs have the same perimeter, their exterior wall and foundation costs are the same. This means that area and the interior walls are the only variables to consider.

   e. Predict which of your designs is the most cost-effective to build, and explain your reasoning.
   Responses will vary, but should note that since the exterior wall expenses represent the greatest cost and they are constant for each area possibility, the additional floor area will cost more, but the cost per square foot will decrease. Students might also note that the maximum area for a polyomino with P = 14 units is 12 square units, yielding the least cost per square foot, and therefore, being the most cost-effective.

Cottage Choices

Cottage Costs

Cottage Area (sq. ft)	Walls	Floor	Roof	Total Cost	Cost per Sq. Ft.
6 216	$11,760	$2,106	$3,159	$17,025	$79
7 252	$11,760	$2,457	$3,686	$17,903	$71
8 288	$11,760	$2,808	$4,212	$18,780	$65
9 324	$11,760	$3,159	$4,739	$19,658	$61
10 360	$11,760	$3,510	$5,265	$20,535	$57
11 396	$11,760	$3,861	$5,792	$21,413	$54
12 432	$11,760	$4,212	$6,318	$22,290	$52

4. Using the data from your table on cottage costs:

   a. Prepare a graph comparing area to total cost. Describe the shape of the graph and the relationship it shows between area and total cost.

   The graph is a straight line, and it shows a constant rate of change between the area and the total cost.

   b. Prepare a second graph comparing area to cost per square foot. Describe the shape of the graph and the relationship it shows between area and cost per square foot.

   The graph is a curve that is slowly decreasing. It shows that as the area increases, the cost per square foot is decreasing, but not at a constant rate.

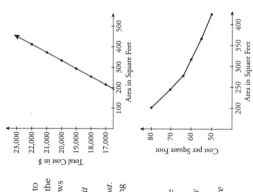

Cottage Choices

5. What do the graphs and the table show about the relationship between area, total cost, and cost per square foot?

   Responses will vary, but may include a) For every additional tile, or 36 square feet of area, the total cost increases by $877, and b) though the cost per square foot continues to decrease as the area increases, the differences in costs per square foot are also decreasing.

6. Describe the best polyomino shape for a cottage design with a perimeter of 14 tile units, and explain your reasoning.

   Responses will vary.

Design Dilemmas

1. Use the square tiles to design various polyomino floor plans for cottages with an area of 8 square units that have a perimeter of 14 units.
   a. Sketch on grid paper several of these designs, making sure that each one is different from the others.
   b. How many different floor plans are there that fit this description? Explain your procedures for determining this.
   Explanations will vary. The 21 possibilities are shown on page 60.
   c. What do you know about the cost of building each of these cottages? Explain your reasoning.
   Because they have the same area and perimeter, they have the same construction costs excluding the interior wall expenses.
   d. Which design do you prefer? Why? Is it livable?
   Responses will vary.

2. a. What is the most cost-effective perimeter for a polyomino with an area of 8 square units? Explain your reasoning.
   The most cost-effective perimeter is 12 units. Explanations will vary, but may suggest this is true because the maximum number of edges are connected and the shape approaches a square.
   b. Sketch different polyomino floor plans on grid paper for 8-square-unit cottages that have the least perimeter.
   c. How many different building plans exist with these specifications? Explain your reasoning.
   There are two plans possible. Explanations will vary, but may include that the number of interior points must be three for the maximum number of edges to be connected.
   d. Which of these designs do you prefer? Why?
   Responses will vary.
   e. How do the costs to build these cottages compare with those in question 1?
   These cottages will cost less, because they have less perimeter, which represents the most expensive aspect of construction.

Design Dilemmas

3. a. What is the most cost-effective area for a polyomino with a perimeter of 14 units? Explain your reasoning.
   12 square units. Explanations will vary, but may include that it has the maximum number of joining edges, resulting in six interior points. They may also note that this is a rectangle whose dimensions differ by 1, representing the minimum perimeter for an area of 12 square units.
   b. How many different cottage plans exist with these specifications? Explain your reasoning.
   Only one. Explanations will vary, but may suggest that rearranging tiles while maintaining the six interior points does not alter the shape.
   c. Compare the construction costs with those for the cottages in questions 1 and 2.
   Because it has the same perimeter with a greater area, this cottage will cost more to build than the cottages in question 1. Though it is more expensive, it will cost less per square foot to build. Since the cottage in question 3 has more area and more perimeter than the cottage in question 2, it will cost more to build the larger cottage; yet, again, in terms of cost per square foot, it is more cost-effective to build. The cottage in question 2 has the same area as the cottages in question 1, but it costs less to build as well as less per square foot.

Number	Number of Tiles	Unit Perimeter	Area (sq. ft)	Perimeter (ft)	Total Cost	Cost per Sq. Ft
1.	8	14	288	84	$18,780	$65
2.	8	12	288	72	$17,100	$59
3.	12	14	432	84	$22,290	$52

4. State several reasons why an architect might be interested in the information developed in questions 1, 2, and 3.
   Responses will vary.

Pitch and Span

As a group, you will complete at least two different roof designs with a 2-foot overhang for your model and choose the type that best suits your cabin. After building a gable roof, your group may select another roof style to construct from the guidelines provided or create your own design.

A gable roof consists of two sloping rectangles called *roof panels* that meet at the ridge. The triangles formed at opposite ends of the cabin are called *gables*.

1. Outline a best-fit rectangle that encloses your cabin floor plan. The best-fit rectangle forms the base of the roof.

   a. Is there more than one possible best-fit rectangle? Explain.
   No. The best-fit rectangle encloses the entire floor plan. To do this, its width is equal to the widest dimension of the floor plan and its length is equal to the longest dimension.

   b. How did your group determine the best-fit rectangle?
   Responses will vary.

2. Gables are usually constructed on the shortest sides of the best-fit rectangle. The width of this side of the cabin is called the *span* of the cabin.

   a. Determine the span of your model.
   Responses will vary.

   b. Half the span is called the *run*. What is the measure of the run for your model?
   Responses will vary.

   c. Compute the actual span and run of your cabin.
   Responses will vary.

Pitch and Span

3. The height of the gable is called the *vertical rise*. The *pitch* of a roof refers to its slope and is expressed as the ratio *vertical rise:run*.

   a. What is the vertical rise for a gable with a 1:1 pitch on your cabin? Explain your reasoning.
   Responses will vary.

   b. What is the vertical rise for a gable with a 1:2 pitch on your cabin? Explain your reasoning.
   Responses will vary.

4. Each member of your group is to choose a different pitch from the list below and draw a prospective gable to scale on grid paper for the roof of your model. Let $\frac{1}{4}$ inch = 1 foot.

   a. 1:1 pitch   b. 1:2 pitch   c. 1:3 pitch   d. 1:4 pitch

5. Explain and illustrate how the pitch of a gable affects its vertical rise.
   In a 1:1 pitch, the rise and run are equal in height, and the pitch is at its greatest. As the pitch decreases, so does the vertical rise, though not in a linear fashion. Its greatest decrease is from 1:1 to 1:2. Examples are shown on page 96.

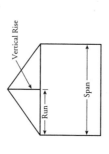

6. Explain how the pitch of a gable affects the cost of the roof.
   As the pitch decreases from 1:1 to 1:4, so does the cost. Since the vertical rise is also decreasing, the area of the triangular gables and the panels, which relate to the amount of roofing material needed and construction time required, is decreasing as well.

7. Cut it out and carefully hold each of the four gables on the appropriate edge of the cabin model for comparison.

   a. Do any appear too tall? Explain.
   Responses will vary.

   b. Do any appear too short? Explain.
   Responses will vary.

   c. Do any appear just right? Explain.
   Responses will vary.

Pitch and Span

8. The ridge angle is formed where the two roof panels meet. Measure the ridge angle for each pitch, using the gables you drew, and record these measures in the table below. Explain how changing the pitch affects the ridge angle.

Ridge Angle

Gable

Pitch	Span	Ridge Angle
1:1	Responses	90°
1:2	will	~128°
1:3	vary.	~142°
1:4		~152°

As the pitch decreas, the right angle increases, but not at a constant rate. It increases by ~38°, then ~14°, then ~10°.

9. Gather data from another group whose model has a different span, and record their ridge angles for the same pitches. If the span changes, what happens to the ridge angle for a pitch of 1:1, 1:2, 1:3, and 1:4? Explain your reasoning.

Pitch	Span	Ridge Angle
1:1	Responses	90°
1:2	will	~128°
1:3	vary.	~142°
1:4		~152°

(Response is continued on next page.)

Pitch and Span

The ridge angles for any given pitch, regardless of the span, are constant. Explanations may vary, but could include that triangles with the same pitch are similar, and similar triangles have the same angle measures.

10. Use your work with gables to answer these questions:
    a. Which slopes seem best for snow? Explain your reasoning.
       Responses will vary, but may include that the steeper pitches are best because the snow will tend to slide off.
    b. Which slopes are not good for snow? Explain your reasoning.
       Responses will vary, but may include that the lower pitches are not good because the snow will build up, and its weight may cause the roof to collapse.

11. Within your group, decide which pitch to use for your gable roof. Explain your selection.
    Responses will vary.

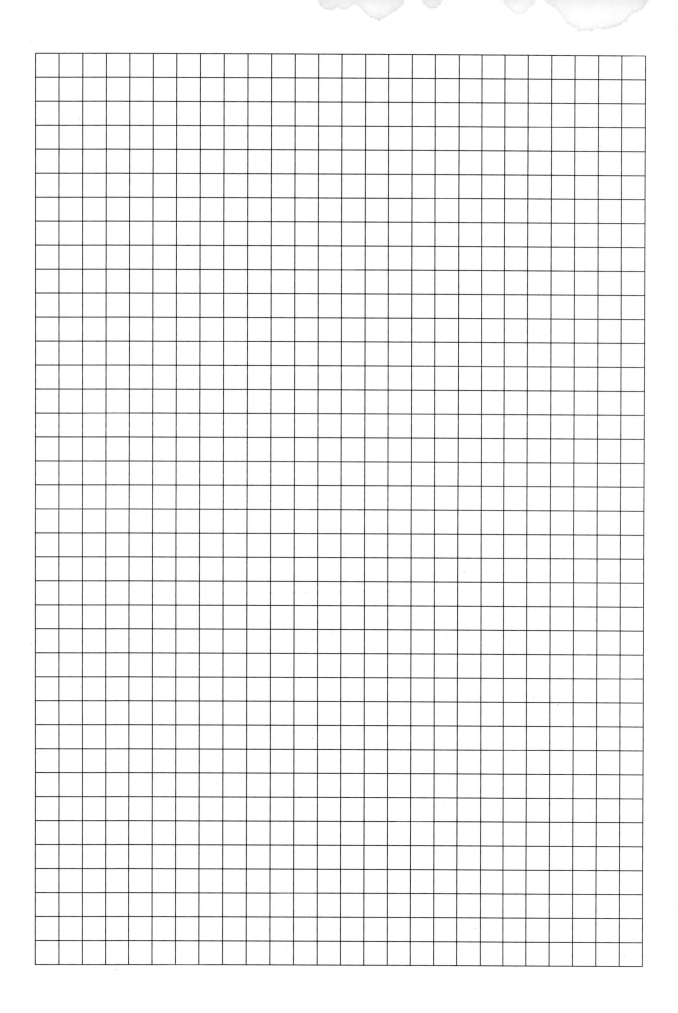